"*Pilgrims and Prisoners* reminded me of the incredible dedication that Ron Nikkel has made to the cause of mercy, justice, and peace in the world by traveling to hundreds of prisons to unconditionally share the love of Jesus. *Pilgrims and Prisoners* gives us a glimpse of the power of Jesus to redeem men and women who society has written off. Any reader will be blessed by this book."

—MICHAEL T. TIMMIS,
author of *Between Two Worlds: The Spiritual Journey of an Evangelical Catholic*

"I have traveled with Ron Nikkel to visit prisons on several continents, and he's one of my heroes. Now he and Andy Corley have served up a rich combination of Jesus-centered wisdom and raw, real-life stories. Jesus emphasized prison outreach in both his first sermon (Luke 4) and one of his last (Matthew 25). I know of no better guides to teach us how to live out that mandate."

—PHILIP YANCEY,
author *Where the Light Fell: A Memoir*

"Ron Nikkel and I walked into prisons in Central America—holes of despair, run by gangs, and for many prisoners, no hope for an exit. It was here I saw Ron light up rooms with his unmistakable understanding, seeding faith and hope. You may never visit a prison, but *Pilgrims and Prisoners* becomes a personal visit into a world neglected and ignored."

—BRIAN C. STILLER,
global ambassador, World Evangelical Alliance

PILGRIMS AND PRISONERS

PILGRIMS AND PRISONERS

When Justice and Mercy Meet

RON NIKKEL
with ANDY CORLEY

Foreword by DAN W. VAN NESS

CASCADE *Books* · Eugene, Oregon

PILGRIMS AND PRISONERS
When Justice and Mercy Meet

Cascade Books
An Imprint of Wipf and Stock Publishers
199 W. 8th Ave., Suite 3
Eugene, OR 97401

www.wipfandstock.com

PAPERBACK ISBN: 978-1-6667-4791-1
HARDCOVER ISBN: 978-1-6667-4792-8
EBOOK ISBN: 978-1-6667-4793-5

Cataloguing-in-Publication data:

Names: Nikkel, Ron, author. | Corley, Andy, author. | Van Ness, Dan W., foreword.
Title: Pilgrims and prisoners : when justice and mercy meet / Ron Nikkel with Andy Corley; foreword by Dan W. Van Ness.
Description: Eugene, OR: Cascade Books, 2023 | Includes bibliographical references and index.
Identifiers: ISBN 978-1-6667-4791-1 (paperback) | ISBN 978-1-6667-4792-8 (hardcover) | ISBN 978-1-6667-4793-5 (ebook)
Subjects: LCSH: Prisoners. | Church work with prisoners. | Prison Fellowship.
Classification: BV4340 .50 2023 (print) | BV4340 (ebook)

JULY 5, 2023 12:46 PM

Dedicated to Ambassador Ivan S. who left position and rank behind to be an Ambassador of Christ, and friend of prisoners.

Without Love there is no Mercy.
Without Mercy there is no Justice.
Without Justice there is no Peace.

Contents

Foreword

FOR THREE YEARS, JESUS and his disciples walked along the dusty roads of Palestine. His parables remind us that he noticed things that can only be seen at a walking pace: how farmers who sow seeds do their work, how a homemaker feels when she finds a coin she had misplaced, how lilies of the fields look when they are in bloom.

I recently saw a video interview with New Testament scholar N. T. Wright,[1] who spoke of the importance of keeping context in mind as we read the New Testament. If we don't, we may unconsciously read it anachronistically—interpreting first-century accounts using twenty-first-century assumptions. For example, Wright mentioned Kosuke Koyama, a Japanese theologian who asserted: "Love has its speed. It is a spiritual speed. It is a different kind of speed from the technological speed to which we are accustomed. It goes on in the depth of our life, whether we notice or not, at three miles an hour. It is the speed we walk and therefore the speed the love of God walks."[2]

You hold in your hands a remarkable book written by a remarkable person. Ron Nikkel has very likely walked through more prisons than anyone else in the world. He served for thirty-two years as president of Prison Fellowship International, a Christian outreach to imprisoned people, the people they are accused of harming, and their families in 120 countries. The prisons were

1. https://www.livegodspeed.org/watchgodspeed-cover.
2. Koyama, *Three Mile an Hour God*, 7.

often overcrowded, filthy paces with little chance of rehabilitating the people living there and with every chance of returning them to their communities more likely to commit new crimes than when they entered. As a lifelong student of the Bible, Ron reflects on what he found as he walked through prisons in light of what the Scriptures say about Jesus, love, justice, righteousness, mercy, and grace. This short book presents his insightful conclusions, made more powerful by the stories he tells of real people he has met in prison. It shows how we who claim to follow Jesus can walk in the footsteps of Jesus.

I had the good fortune of working with Ron for twenty years. He is a great storyteller and a gifted author. His weekly memos to staff were so insightful that for me they became "must read" every Monday morning. Similarly, I found myself marking up this book, eventually reading it devotionally, allowing its message to marinate in my heart.

The love of God, Koyama tells us, moves at a three-mile-an-hour pace. One consequence is that those of us who would much rather drive past a prison than go inside are unable to see what is happening there. If we could only slow down, we would see miracles of grace and justice that are visible only to those who, like Ron and Andy, have followed Jesus into prison.

DAN W. VAN NESS

Preface

ANDY CORLEY AND I first met in Cape Town, South Africa during
a world conference on evangelization. I do not have much interest
in conferences because it seems to me a lot of people are more
given to talking about issues than responding to issues. This is
particularly true when it concerns the challenges of responding to
the poor, the imprisoned, the oppressed, and victimized people—
those who are marginalized in neglected parts of the world and
social order, as well as those who are so often hidden in plain sight.

Andy was a successful British business entrepreneur, and I
was based in Washington, DC as president of Prison Fellowship
International (PFI). Our worlds could not have been more different, yet we discovered each other as brothers in Christ and kindred
spirits. There was an instant bond between us that led to Andy
joining the PFI Board and, several years after I stepped down from
leadership, he became the CEO and president.

However, this book is not about our friendship and partner-
ship in PFI. This book is about what we have discovered in following Jesus into the prisons of the world and reaching out to people
marginalized and overcome by injustice.

Why would anyone care about prisoners and criminal justice
when there are so many other people who are more deserving of
our compassion and help? This is a question rather like the question of the person who asked Jesus, "Who is my neighbor?" Caring for troubled persons, those who are in trouble, and those who
make trouble for others is not based on a continuum of those who

are less deserving and more deserving. Instead, it is based entirely on God's love and mercy for all persons without consideration of who they are, where they are, or what they have done. In fact, God's heart seems more inclined to those who we overlook and deem unworthy.

God's mercy is always undeserved. God's justice is not fulfilled in fair judgment and punishment. God's love knows no limits and touches the world where we least expect to find it or express it. God's righteousness is expressed in Jesus of Nazareth, a Galilean. After John had been imprisoned Scripture says of Jesus, that the people living in darkness beyond the Jordan in Galilee of the Gentiles have seen a great light, dawning on them as those living in the land of the shadow of death.[3]

As followers of Jesus into the underside, the shadowlands of imprisonment, inhumanity, hopelessness, and despair, we are discovering the loving presence and transforming power of God where it is often least expected—among those who are imprisoned.

So why should anyone care? This book attempts to share why God extends his love to "outsiders" and "undeserving" people. God's kingdom is sometimes described as being upside down because its values run counter to human logic and expectations. Chuck Colson often ventured that God is building his kingdom from the bottom up, among prisoners and the most unlikely and forgotten of people.

This might just be the case, but not only because of God's transforming love for those suffer marginalization and rejection, but also because those who dare to meet Jesus among them in the shadowlands of human failure, respectability, and need are changed themselves.

RON NIKKEL AND ANDY CORLEY

3. Matthew 4:12–16.

CHAPTER 1

God in the Margins

AFTER BEING RELEASED FROM PRISON, Chuck Colson, of the infamous Watergate political scandal who went on to found Prison Fellowship, began spending every Easter Sunday in prison—not in a church resounding with joyous Easter pageantry, but in the dreary confinement of prison cells.

The news media were intrigued by this, and reporters asked him why he would rather be in a prison on Easter Sunday than be in church.

Chuck typically responded by saying that there was no place on earth where he would rather celebrate the day of Jesus' resurrection than in a prison—more even than in the most magnificent cathedral with its stained glass, big choir, and people in their finest. He continued:

> If you want to know what Easter is about, then there's no better place to find out than in the tombs of our society, which is what our prisons are. Jesus was resurrected from death in a tomb. On this, of all days, prison is the one place where Jesus is present. Never forget what Jesus said in his first sermon, "The Spirit of the Lord is on me, because he has anointed me to preach good news to the poor. He has sent me to proclaim freedom for the prisoners and recovery of sight for the blind, to release the oppressed."

Inside the prison, the inmates also wonder why a man who was one of the closest advisors to the president of the United States has come to visit them in prison. Sensing their unspoken questions Chuck launched into the story of Jesus' love for prisoners.

> You see, it was radical to proclaim "freedom for the prisoners" in the Roman Empire; nobody cared about prisoners. But Jesus did. And the situation is no different today. Concern for people locked up in this prison is not a popular message. Anyone who preaches this message in one of those nice downtown churches will get the same icy response that Jesus did. The rich and powerful people will run them out of town just like they ran Jesus out of town. Never forget that Jesus died as a prisoner, and he knows what it is like to be in a place like this. He understands everything you are going through.

Colson continued:

> Have you ever been strip-searched, beaten, and mocked? Do any of you know what it is like to have people give false testimony and use fake evidence to trump up the charges against you? Do any of you know what it feels like to have the prosecutors and police use muscle to wrench a guilty plea out of you? Do any of you know what it is like to have one of your closest friends betray you, and friends you thought you could count on abandon you? Well, that is what Jesus went through. There is nothing you have experienced that Jesus doesn't understand, because that is exactly what happened to him; and he is right here in prison with you, because he knows what you are going through, and he loves you!

For most prison inmates, Jesus is someone who belongs to the church, in a safe, comfortable religious setting, not someone who belongs in prison with the likes of them. When Chuck told them about Jesus was often the first time many of them begin to see Jesus differently. Through Chuck's story they saw Jesus not as someone who was too good for them, unconcerned about them, or angry with them. Rather, they saw that Jesus cared about them and was present with them because he understood and related to them in the depths of loneliness, darkness, and imprisonment; because he had been there.

JESUS, THE GALILEAN FROM NAZARETH

From the very beginning Jesus is marked as an outsider by the religious establishment of the day. He hails from Nazareth, a small town characterized by the prophet Isaiah as being in the region called "Galilee of the Gentiles."[1]

Nazareth is the hometown of Jesus' mother Mary and where she and Joseph settle when they return from exile in Egypt. Jesus is raised in Nazareth, a small village in Galilee. Nazareth is where he begins his public ministry. The Gospel of Luke describes Jesus returning to his hometown as an adult, to give what is commonly thought of as the inaugural address at the beginning of his ministry. This occurs shortly after his baptism and wilderness temptation.

> Jesus returned to Galilee in the power of the Spirit . . . He went to Nazareth, where he had been brought up, and on the Sabbath day he went into the synagogue, as was his custom. He stood up to read, and the scroll of the prophet Isaiah was handed to him. Unrolling it, he found the place where it is written: "The Spirit of the Lord is on me, because he has anointed me to proclaim good news to the poor. He has sent me to proclaim freedom for the prisoners and recovery of sight for the blind, to set the oppressed free, to proclaim the year of the Lord's favor."[2]

It is by no accident or mere coincidence that Jesus comes from Nazareth, and that much of his ministry embraces the towns and villages of "Galilee of the Gentiles." At the time, the region was geographically distanced from mainstream Jewish culture and religion, which centered on the temple of Jerusalem, in Judea. Galilee is sandwiched between the non-Jewish territory of Samaria and the Hellenistic settlements of the Decapolis.[3] It is a region of mixed

---

1. Isaiah 9:1, 2.
2. Luke 4:14(a),16–19 (see also Isaiah 61:1, 2).
3. The Decapolis was a region comprising ten cities. Those cities and the

races, cultures, and religion and Nazareth is situated in proximity to two cities of the Decapolis, Tiberias and Sepphoris.

Because of this social and cultural environment, Judean Jews tend to look down on Galilean Jews for lacking proper religious piety and purity. Their manner of speech is considered sloppy because of the distinctive Aramaic dialect and accent which is, to their ears, uncultured and inferior. Even very devout Galilean Jewish believers are regarded as inferior, not sophisticated like the cultured Jews of Jerusalem.

Not only is Galilee regarded with a measure of contempt by Judean Jews, but with Nazareth being a largely Jewish village in a Gentile region, it is also looked down on by its Gentile Galilean neighbors. This relegates the people of Nazareth to being outsiders among their Galilean neighbors as well as to their fellow Jews.

John's account of Nathanael's response to Philip's inviting him to meet Jesus reflects the low esteem that even Jewish Galileans had for their own people. Nathanael's response is totally dismissive of any possibility that Jesus could be the Messiah. He is from Nazareth, after all! When Philip finds Nathanael, he says, "We have found the one Moses wrote about in the Law, and about whom the prophets also wrote—Jesus of Nazareth, the son of Joseph."

"Nazareth! Can anything good come from there?" exclaims Nathanael.[4]

John tells of another occasion when Jesus is speaking to people gathered in the temple courts at Jerusalem. Among those who hear Jesus that day, many respond dismissively just because of his Galilean roots. They see him as a person who cannot possibly be God's promised Messiah. It is altogether obvious to them that he hails from the wrong side of the tracks. "On hearing his words, some of the people said, 'Surely this man is the Prophet.' Others said, 'He is the Messiah.' Still others asked, 'How can the Messiah come from Galilee?'"[5]

---

surrounding region were largely predominantly inhabited by Gentiles and were culturally defined by Greek influence.

4. John 1:45–46.

5. John 7:40–41.

THE MOST UNLIKELY MESSIAH

One might think that Jesus' announcement in his hometown syna-gogue would have been met with sustained applause—but it was not. Instead, their applause culminates in anger and the people rise up to run him out of town. Their initial amazement at his eloquent speech quickly turns hostile when they realize who he is and what he is saying. How could one of their own have the audacity to sug-gest that he is the fulfillment of Isaiah's prophecy? Who does Jesus think he is?!

What fuels their anger even more is Jesus' pointed remark that, during the great famine, God did not send the prophet Elijah to help one of the many widows in Israel, but to help a non-Jewish widow in Zarephath—an outsider. As if there weren't widows in Israel far more deserving than a Gentile widow! And then Jesus draws attention to Naaman, a Syrian military officer who God healed through the prophet Elisha, though none of the many people with leprosy in Israel were healed during that time.

The people are incensed. How could this possibly be? It is preposterous to think that God would have mercy on foreign overlords, instead of giving preferential treatment and priority consideration to his own suffering people. This is not what the God-fearing people of Nazareth want to hear. They are expecting God's promised salvation and deliverance to be for them, to de-liver them from Roman rule and oppression, from subservience to Gentiles and from being outsiders even among their fellow Jews. Implying that God puts undeserving foreigners ahead of their own people is insulting enough. But that this is being said by Jesus adds insult to the injury they feel. After all, they know where Jesus comes from and who he really is. His parents are Joseph and Mary, uneducated, working-class people just like them. They remember the questionable legitimacy of Jesus' birth and do not see Jesus as having a godly, respectable pedigree. He wasn't even born in a nor-mal place, but in a stable used to shelter animals.

When the realization of Jesus' background dawns on them, they are furious and chase him from the synagogue, propelling him out of the town to push him off a cliff. There is simply no way that Jesus is the man from God. They know that God will send a Messiah of substance, someone able to powerfully turn the tables on their abusers and their enemies. It is ludicrous, indeed blasphemous, to think that God's Messiah will come from anywhere but a place of higher power and influence. The Messiah will surely come in glory, ordained by God with political might and authority to restore the rule of David. The promised deliverer won't look anything like Jesus of Nazareth—an ordinary and most unlikely character from Galilee of the Gentiles living with them on the margins of Jewish respectability.

Jesus is a most unlikely person indeed. He was born to an unmarried woman under unseemly circumstances. He grows up in an "backwater" rural town. His manner of life as a carpenter's son seems utterly unbefitting that of the Messiah. Even his closest companions assume that if Jesus really is the God-ordained Messiah, he will eventually show himself with power and authority to raise Israel out of from Roman occupation and subservience.

In addition to Jesus being born to Mary and Joseph, her fiancé, his family origins are anything but pure. His family tree listed in Matthew's Gospel is not a straight, pure Jewish lineage. Four women are included in the family tree of Jesus forebears. Each of them happens to be an alien Gentile woman. This is a scandal to religious purists for whom genealogy is the basis for determining the purity of a person's lineage and Jewish heritage. The inclusion of women in Matthew's genealogy is problematic enough without drawing attention to four Gentile women—Tamar of Canaan, Rahab the harlot from Jericho, Ruth a Moabitess, and Bathsheba the defiled widow of Uriah, a Hittite. Jesus' roots include people on the margins of acceptability, unlikely people of impure origins.

A CAST OF UNLIKELY CHARACTERS

Evading the hostile intent of his hometown people in Nazareth, Jesus continues to other towns and villages in Galilee and assembles a group of unlikely men to follow him. Those he chooses to be his companions are not selected for their education or their status or standing in the community. Instead, they are a motley crew of fishermen, nationalist extremists (zealots), traitorous tax collectors, and very ordinary people. Luke (in the Acts of the Apostles) describes them as being unschooled and ordinary men.[6] Jesus could not have chosen a more unlikely group of companions to join him in proclaiming and demonstrating the presence of God's kingdom.

Accompanied by these men, Jesus spends most of his time proclaiming the good news of the kingdom in the towns and villages of Galilee. His primary audience seems to be among the marginalized people of Israel and even extends to the Samaritans, the historically estranged descendants of Jewish ancestry, despised as a spiritually corrupted, mixed race of Israelites and pagan foreigners. Consistent with his proclamation in the synagogue of Nazareth, Jesus' ministry embraces the poor, the sick, and those who are oppressed and captive—people who are marginalized and looked down on by Israel's religious leaders and devout believers.

It is among the people in Galilee of the Gentiles that Jesus, accompanied by his unlikely companions, begins proclaiming the good news of God's kingdom and demonstrating its presence. Six hundred years before Jesus, Isaiah pointed to this saying: "There will be no more gloom for those who were in distress . . . he will honor Galilee of the nations, by the Way of the Sea, beyond the Jordan. The people walking in darkness have seen a great light; on those living in the land of deep darkness a light has dawned."[7] The impact of Jesus' ministry is light and life coming to a people lost in the shadowlands of human alienation and insignificance.

JESUS, SIGN OF GOD'S KINGDOM

What is so significant about Jesus' identification with the marginalized people among whom he proclaims the good news of God's kingdom?

6. Acts 4:13.
7. Isaiah 9:1a, 2.

It is in our human nature to expect that political, economic, social, and even spiritual change on a national or global level will only be accomplished through power, money, and influence at the highest level. Certainly, that was the prevailing expectation during Jesus' time. They expected God's kingdom would come in power and glory to restore the fortunes of Israel and to set things right for their people. In that respect, it is understandable that Jesus of Nazareth did not fit their worldview or their expectations for the Messiah.

If we are honest, this response to someone like Jesus is completely normal. Who would expect Almighty God to bring redemption and salvation, to establish his kingdom through a person who spends his time among the marginalized, outcast, powerless, and oppressed? However, God's kingdom is not dependent on our paradigms of power politics, our strategic planning, economic leverage, and metrics of success. God's kingdom has a different foundation, and the values of God's kingdom are usually the opposite of our own.

It is the poor and the meek, the merciful and the peacemakers, even the mournful and the persecuted who Jesus proclaims as being blessed. The good news Jesus brings and demonstrates is redemption and restoration for the poor, the prisoners, the blind (the disabled and disadvantaged), those who are looked down on, and those who suffer oppression.

It takes the disciples a long time to understand the significance of what Jesus represents. When they ask Jesus to tell them what they should expect and look for in the coming of the kingdom, he tells them several stories. In the final story Jesus describes the kingdom as a place where God welcomes those who touch Jesus, those languishing on the margins of society with compassion and respect—feeding him among the hungry, giving drink to him through the thirsty, providing welcome and hospitality to him through strangers, clothing him through the naked, caring for him through the sick, and visiting him through prisoners.[8]

How does this make any sense?

8. Matthew 25:31–46.

It is in responding to people on the margins, those who are socially, politically, and economically left out, left behind, and left alone, that we come face-to-face with Jesus—who himself knows what it is like to live on the margins, to be an outsider. If we do not get the significance of Jesus' identity as a Galilean, marginalized by the Jewish elite and his own neighbors, we will miss the point of the radically good news of God the Father's love inherent in the life and teachings of Jesus of Nazareth. Jesus was sent by God into the depths of our human condition and experience of alienation, and if we do not meet him there, we most likely miss him completely.

SO WHAT?

It has been said that "the true measure of any society can be found in how it treats its most vulnerable members."[9] Nelson Mandela went a step further by observing that "no one truly knows a nation until one has been inside its jails. A nation should not be judged by how it treats its highest citizens, but its lowest ones."[10]

While observations like this reflect an impulse to justice and compassion in the heart of human society, that impulse is seldom acted on. What we "know" to be right and good most often is not how the world works. Jesus shows that the heart of God for offenders, those judged unfit and unworthy, and people on the margins, goes beyond mere sentiment and good will.

Chuck Colson often told the following anecdote when addressing prison inmates.

> You know, nobody outside really cares about you being in this prison—but Jesus does. I often tell the good people in church, "You need to come with me to prison." They are shocked and say "no, no, don't you know those are bad and dangerous people in there?" And then I will

9. Generally attributed to Mohandas Gandhi, leader in the independence movement of India under British colonial rule

10. In December 2015, the UN General Assembly adopted a revision of the "United Nations Standard Minimum Rules for the Treatment of Prisoners." This revision is known as "the Nelson Mandela Rules."

ask them, "But you want to go to heaven, don't you?" Then they all smile and nod their heads saying, "Yes, of course we do." "Well," I tell them, "then you better get used to being with prisoners now, because one of the first people you will meet in heaven is a prisoner—the criminal who was executed on the cross next to Jesus! He is the only person Jesus ever promised to have a place in heaven with him."[11]

Significantly, one of the first persons Jesus invites into his inner circle of companions is Levi, a tax collector.[12] Like his fellow tax collectors, Levi is a Jew enlisted by the Romans to collect taxes from his fellow Jews. His fellow Jews despise him for this. Collaborating with the Gentile Romans makes him a sinner and a traitor in the eyes of his own people. He is despised and reviled, shunned for being unrighteous and morally compromised.[13] Yet Jesus does not shun Levi. Instead, he invites Levi to follow him, then joins him and his fellow tax collectors for dinner. When the religious leaders notice that Jesus is eating with tax collectors and sinners they are indignant. How can a righteous man deign to partake at the same table with Levi and his ilk?

In response to their criticism, Jesus says, "It is not the healthy who need a doctor, but the sick. I have not come to call the righteous, but sinners to repentance."[14]

Associating with and caring for disreputable and reprehensible people does not sully Jesus' character in the least. Rather, by doing so he is demonstrating God's love and mercy for people on the margins of moral purity, social respectability, and religious piety. That is why God came down to humanity in the person Jesus of Nazareth, in Galilee of the Gentiles.

11. Ron Nikkel journal notes from prison visits with Chuck Colson.

12. Luke 5:27–31; Mark 2:13–17.

13. See Jesus' parable about the Pharisee and the tax collector in Luke 18:9–14.

14. Luke 5:31–32.

CHAPTER 2

The Face of God

Beyond a Mirror Image

In Jesus of Nazareth, God shows a human face, entering humanity from the bottom of the social order, not as royalty or elite, but as an ordinary human being among a least likely people living in difficult circumstances. God could have chosen to reveal himself anywhere and in any manner, yet chose to engage humanity as a human—and not just any human, but as a poor and powerless individual in a marginalized community of politically oppressed people. So, Jesus enters the human race, not as one among the ruling class or elite, but among a people who are despised, rejected, and subservient, proving that God meets, respects, and dignifies all of humanity by his love.

The good news of God in Jesus is that every person matters to God, not just those who are typically considered worthy and significant. This should not be surprising to anyone because God is the Creator of every human being and values each one. From the beginning, Genesis asserts that human beings were created by God in his own image.[1] God invests himself and reveals himself in human beings as the epitome of his creation. Every single human "face" bears the image of God. By becoming incarnate in Jesus

---

1. Genesis 1:26–27.

of Nazareth, God shows that there are no limits to the depth and extent of his love for humans, whatever their place or status.

THE FACE OF EDDIE

Eddie is a young man serving his eighth or ninth prison sentence. He cannot remember a time when he was not in trouble. His family background is sordid, one of deep poverty, abuse, and violence. Eddie fell into alcohol and drug abuse when he was just a kid. It was his only way of escaping reality and dulling the pain of being unwanted. As a result, he has no education and no work skills or basic work habits. It is difficult for him to get a job, much less keep one. So, Eddie's life has been miserable, and reflects the lives of many young men and women who are unloved, neglected, and abused. He steals whatever he can sell or trade, and sometimes his own body, to obtain the illicit drugs or pills or booze he craves. He often becomes violent and abusive toward others and tends to create problems wherever he goes. Nobody wants anything to do with Eddie, and nobody knows what to do with him other than to lock him up in prison. He has no friends, and his family has completely abandoned him.

Eddie knows misery and yearns for a better life. But every time he is released from prison and resolves to walk a good path, he ends up in the same old place. Without supportive friends, a place to live, or a job, he falls into the same behavior patterns, doing the same things just to survive the "hell" of his life all over again. He feels rotten but is unable to help himself. He has pretty much given up trying to be good.

"Do you think God loves me, even when I fall?" he asks the chaplain one day.

From his pained expression and downcast eyes it is obvious that Eddie does not think he is good enough for God. He is not even good enough for his own family. Everyone has rejected him. He doesn't have a single friend.

Anyone looking into Eddie's face, marred with crude prison tattoos, or reading his lengthy criminal record, will find it difficult to see anything that is attractive about him. By any social measure he is repulsive, unlikeable—impossible to love. Everyone who has tried to help him and is familiar with his story has written him off as not being worth the time and effort to help. He is considered a hopeless case, an incorrigible offender. There is no doubt that Eddie will keep on committing crimes until he comes to a self-destructive if not violent end. Perhaps, if he is lucky, the justice system will eventually lock him up for good, for his own protection.

Eddie's question echoes in the background. "Can God still love me, even when I fall?" Well meaning people have responded to Eddie, "Of course God loves you, just repent and turn to him in faith."

Eddie yearns to believe that someone cares about him, but it is impossible for him to believe that God really loves him when he keeps on failing and causing trouble. Even the other inmates in prison don't like him. No one cares if he lives or dies. When Eddie looks at himself in the mirror and sees his own face, all he sees is a person called scum, worthless, user, habitual offender, a lost cause. He is barely twenty years old and very much on the margins of society, socially and psychologically considered beyond help and hope.

But the question is, what does God see, when God looks at Eddie's scarred and unattractive face? God knows far more about the condition of Eddie's life and criminal record than anyone else. So, what does God think about Eddie? How does God respond to Eddie's question, "Does God still love me even when I fail?"

ALL GOD'S CHILDREN

During the apostle Paul's first visit to Athens, he is struck by the panoply of gods that the Athenians have fashioned for themselves. They are so inclusive that they have even erected a monument to the unknown God, just in case they might have missed something. Instead of criticizing and condemning the people of Athens for their idolatry, Paul affirms them as having dignity and worth in relationship to God—God, their Creator who they do not know, for he is the one who "gives everyone life and breath and everything else . . . For in him we live and move and have our being . . . We are his offspring."[2]

Paul's message to the Athenians is that God not only sees the life of every person but is the source of life. Each person is God-created, and their life is God-given. Human life is God's special design, not just for the first human beings who were called Adam and Eve, but for every human being since then that has come into the world because of God's creative act.

> In the beginning God said, "Let us make man in our im-age, in our likeness, and let them rule over the fish of the sea and the birds of the air, over the livestock, over all the earth, and over all the creatures that move along the ground." So, God created man in his own image, in the image of God he created him; male and female he created them.[3]

When the psalmist reflects on his own life, he sees something that Eddie is unable to see in the prison mirror, and what others do not see when they look into Eddie's face or read his record.

> You created my inmost being; you knit me together in my mother's womb. I praise you because I am fearfully and wonderfully made; your works are wonderful, I know that full well. My frame was not hidden from you when I was made in the secret place, when I was woven together in the depths of the earth. Your eyes saw my unformed body; all the days ordained for me were written in your book before one of them came to be.[4]

Human life originates from the creative action of God and thus human beings have ever been and ever will be in a special relationship with the Creator. As the Creator of each person, God endows each person with dignity. Every single person is inherently part of the human family created by God. No person exists outside

2. Acts 17:25–28.
3. Genesis 1:26–27.
4. Psalm 139:13–16.

of the human family. Anyone seeing themselves in the mirror will see a person uniquely created by God. Anyone looking into the face of another person will see not just another human being, but a person created by God in God's own image. The significance of each person being made in the image of God is acknowledged by James in the simplicity of how people speak to and about other people. "With the tongue we praise our Lord and Father, and with it we curse human beings, who have been made in God's likeness. Out of the same mouth come praise and cursing. My brothers and sisters, this should not be."[5]

By cursing, demeaning, condemning, and writing off another person we essentially marginalize, demean, condemn, and write off not just that person, but the One who has given life and who loves that person. The inherent dignity and value of Eddie is not a function of attractive appearance, personal reputation, or the despicable and destructive deeds he may have committed. Nothing can erase his God-given worth and dignity. Each person is created by God and their dignity and worth are God-endowed, not self-made.

IMAGO DEI

So, what does it mean for a person to be made in the image and likeness of God? It obviously does not mean a physical resemblance to God or that God's face looks anything like our human faces. Rather it means that God has bestowed human beings with honor that he has not bestowed on other creatures or even the sum total of all creation. God formed humankind from the dust of the ground and then, by God's infusion of "the breath of life" the first human became a living being.[6]

What we humans have in common with every other animal is the created world of trees and flowers, seas and mountains, trees, and deserts. We belong to God's creation, having been formed from

5. James 3:9–10.
6. Genesis 2:7.

the dust of the ground. However, what sets us apart from the rest of creation is our unique union with God, the "breath of God" by which we were given life. We are different from other creatures. In addition to being endowed with physical life, we are endowed with spiritual life by God's breath within us. Although genetically we are remarkably like chimpanzees, with our DNA being 99 percent the same as that of a chimpanzee, there is a vast difference between humans and chimpanzees (and the rest of the animal kingdom).

Traces of the divine are reflected in our human nature in that we have a sense of infinity—the existence of things beyond time and space like justice, truth, beauty, and love. At a deeper level, the image of God is reflected in our spiritual nature as persons endowed with conscience, moral reasoning, along with a bent and capacity to know God that we express in spiritual quest, religious devotion, and worship. Human nature is inherently creative, thoughtful, artistic, moral, relational, hungry for meaning and purpose.

Another way of understanding the image of God in human beings is reflected in the representative role that God gave to humans, "to rule over the fish of the sea and the birds of the air, over the livestock, over all the earth, and over all the creatures that move along the ground."[7] Thus, the image of God in humanity is reflected in the role and responsibility given to humanity as God's representatives in creation. The psalmist eloquently summarizes this high status of being human. Nothing in all of Creation has higher status than a human person.

> What is mankind that you are mindful of them,
>   human beings that you care for them?
> You have made them a little lower than the angels
>   and crowned them with glory and honor.
> You made them rulers over the works of your hands;
>   you put everything under their feet.[8]

---

7. Genesis 1:26–27.
8. Psalm 8:4–6.

16

THE LIKENESS OF GOD DEFACED

As beings made in the image of God, bearing God's likeness means that human life is sacred. A person's worth is not inherent in their personality, status, stature, accomplishment, education, religion, culture, or even behavior. Every person's worth, without exception, is established by the fact that God created human life in unique relationship to himself. Therefore, the life of every individual, even a person like Eddie, is precious and of sacred worth, not because it is something a person earns or achieves but fundamentally because each person is endowed with worth by God from the beginning of their lives.

Of course, we sometimes have difficulty recognizing and appreciating our own worth and the worth of others. When Adam and Eve turned away from God by disobeying him, they saw their naked inadequacy and vulnerability, so they tried to cover themselves up and hide from God. Through them all of humanity lost face before God and became disconnected from him and each other. Adam blamed Eve, and Eve blamed the serpent. The tendency to cover up, hide, and blame has been part of our human condition ever since. Eddie blames his family, the unfairness of life, and the injustice of the system. He has often lied to cover up his misdeeds, he has tried to run and hide, and he seeks escape through drugs and alcohol. His life is so tarnished and misshapen that it does not sparkle with God-given dignity and worth.

People tell Eddie that he is "no good" and worthless by distancing, demeaning, and damning him. Whether by his own fault or the fault of others, Eddie is not living up to the good that God created him for. People who encounter Eddie treat him like human garbage, not like a young man made in the image of God. Neither Eddie nor the people who look down on him respect the sanctity of human life. By disrespecting oneself and disrespecting others, people disrespect God who made them both.

Of course, Eddie is responsible for his behavior, and certainly those who mistreated him as a child also bear responsibility. However, neither individual behavior nor the fall of humankind into sin and evil nullifies the image of God in a person. Yet we wonder about people like Eddie, who seem so incorrigible. We wonder about mass killers, and tyrants who commit horrible acts of violence against others. Is it possible for anyone to lose or destroy the image of God imprinted in their lives from birth?

This is a troubling question. It can help for us to understand the difference between the *imago Dei* in terms of a person's inherent human worth and how that worth is expressed by their life. The *imago Dei* is God-given and therefore can neither be created nor negated by human edicts or actions. It is God-given. However, by complicity in evil and sin persons can obscure, distort, and disfigure the good that they were created for. This does not change the fact that they were created by God for good, and there is nothing that a person can do to eradicate the God-given sanctity and dignity of their own lives or the life of another. The image of God does not mean that a person is endowed with moral and spiritual perfection. Instead, Scripture reveals that the image of God remains because it is from God, and not a function of or dependent on a person's behavior, lifestyle, or character. Sin does separate a person in relationship to God, but does not separate a person from the unalterable reality of being made in God's image and being loved by God.

As difficult as it is to see the image of God reflected in Eddie's face or in his behavior, Eddie is fully a human being created by God. Because of this reality the only answer to Eddie's question is, "Yes, Eddie. God has loved you from the beginning and totally loves you, even when you fall."

GOD IN HUMAN LIKENESS

A memorable quote attributed to Voltaire states, "In the beginning God created man in his own image, and man has been trying to repay the favor ever since." Fundamentally this speaks to our human tendency of trying to "best" God by trying to be God, using our God-given freedom of will to please ourselves, to run our own lives the way we choose, and to judge others as being worthy or unworthy. From the beginning, the heart of human temptation has been to usurp the place of God. The story of the fall of humankind (the divine disconnect) portrays the serpent saying, "God knows that when you eat the [forbidden fruit] your eyes will be opened and you will be like God, knowing good and evil." And seeing that the tree was good for food and pleasing to the eye, and desirable for gaining wisdom those first humans ate. "Then the eyes of both of them were opened, and they realized that they were naked; so they sewed fig leaves together and made coverings for themselves."[9]

From that time forward the story of God and humanity has been the story of God working to draw willful, wayward humanity back into relationship, not by coercion or force but through his patient, merciful, generous, unending love for humanity. Some have likened this to God redemptively placing humankind back in the garden of Eden so they can be born anew, as if for the very first time. God knows the very worst of Eddie and of each person, yet regards each person as his own. In Jesus of Nazareth the story of salvation culminates with God affirming the dignity and worth of human beings by becoming one of them in love—not to condemn them for sin and evil but to rescue and restore them.

The Gospel of John opens with this amazing declaration, "In the beginning was the Word and the Word was with God, and the Word was God . . . Through him all things were made; without him nothing was made that has been made . . . The Word became flesh and made his dwelling among us."[10]

After the creation of human life, no act of God is more significant than God humbling himself out of his great love for humanity, to become one of us, to rescue us and set all things right that have been so horribly marred and misshapen by sin, to redeem and restore the defilement and defacement of humanity. God's embrace of the world in Jesus Christ is the good news of redemption and salvation for all people, including those considered most unlikely and unworthy.

9. Genesis 3:5–7.
10. John 1:1–3, 14.

This is the good news of God's kingdom, the good news of God's love for Eddie, to the end that Eddie might be forgiven, restored, and the image of God fully realized in his life. "For God so loved the world that he gave his one and only Son, that whoever believes in him shall not perish but have eternal life. For God did not send his Son into the world to condemn the world, but to save the world through him."[11]

Given the stark reality of our human depravity and complicity in all kinds of evil, why would God turn his face toward us? What does God's "face" look like, that he would stoop to the margins and the gutters of human existence to embrace the likes of Eddie and all those who, despite bearing his image, are pushed aside, put down, condemned, written off, and judged unworthy human beings?

11. John 3:16–17.

CHAPTER 3

The Love of God

Beyond Skin Deep

"I DON'T NEED YOU or anyone to tell me about God's love," snarls Yuri.

"I was suffering in prison with no justice and God did not help me. So do not say he cares about me. But—see, I believe in God!"

With that Yuri, a Russian prisoner who was just released from the prison, rips open his shirt, thumps his chest, and points to the large tattoo of a crucifix. "I believe there is God but he does nothing to help me!"

For Yuri, as for many prisoners during Soviet times, his tattoo was more a statement of protest against the oppressive regime than a statement of faith. Now that he is finally free, that tattoo is still his badge of honor for having survived the system, but that is just about all he really wants of God.

Father Bezmenov stands by quietly as Yuri rails against God and rails against the system. He nods his head thoughtfully, his kindly eyes looking into Yuri's face.

"I see that you have God on your chest," he says as Yuri's tirade fades, "but is he in your heart? God loves you and wants a relationship with you that is more than a skin-deep tattoo."

KNOWING GOD

Like Yuri, many people believe in the existence of an impersonal God, but one who is not personally concerned with them. Some know a great deal about God but have no relational connection with God. It is one thing for them to know about God, quite another to know God.

To know God personally involves a relationship with God that is more than superficial, or a vague belief in God's existence. Since the creation of humanity in his own image, God's desire is for human beings to flourish in relationship with him. Scripture tells the story of God's relationship with humankind and records the saga of human self-interest, attempts to create and worship gods of human making, and the will to live life independently from God the Creator. Nevertheless, God persists in loving the people he created in his own image with no exceptions. God's relationship with humankind and love for each person is more than skin deep.

The history of humanity is a story of repeated twists and turns, ups and downs evidencing the futility and folly of their attempts to supplant God in their affections and to eliminate God from daily life. Time and again God takes the initiative to draw humanity back into relationship with himself. It does not take the Israelites long to turn their backs on God after he liberates them from Egyptian slavery. As soon as they face obstacles and deprivation, they become impatient and grumble about God, who does not meet their expectations. So, they craft a god of their own design—a beautiful golden calf that they can see and admire. And though they turn their backs on God, he does not write them off or abandon them. Instead, God reaches out to them to establish an agreement (covenant) with them, to draw them into a mutual relationship in which he will be with them, guide them, and provide for them. They simply have to trust that God will guide them for good. He will be their God, and they will be his people.

GOD BUILDS WITH "REJECTS"

Using its totalitarian power, the Soviet Union attempted to create a society without God. In many respects it succeeded in eradicating God from public life. Religion was relegated to superstition and outlawed, replaced with the ideals of scientific socialism. After being imprisoned for his criticism of the Soviet system, Aleksandr Solzhenitsyn observed that the claims of Soviet atheistic ideology fell far short of perfecting humanity. Over time, as the majority of its people forgot God, corruption became endemic, and the highest ideals of Sovietism and the building of a just and equitable society were crumbling.

Although the state disavowed God altogether and the people turned their backs on God, God did not forget or discard the Soviet people. It was among unlikely inmates in the gulag labor camps, and among poor peasants, exiled poets, and elderly *babushkas* that God made his presence felt. These marginalized people turned to God in hope and faith because they knew that only God was with them. God, in his love, embraced maligned and overlooked men and women, nourishing them in faith and building his kingdom within the Soviet Empire. Many inmates like Yuri knew hardly anything about God, yet they somehow sensed that God was present and helping them survive the repressive Soviet regime. Among them were some whose relationship with God went so deep that their faith was regarded as a threat by the state. For that very reason they had been imprisoned. Ironically, in prison that faith sustained them, and they shared their faith in God with other prisoners.

Recounting his own imprisonment in the Soviet gulags, Solzhenitsyn tells the gripping story of how the faith of Boris Kornfeld, an imprisoned doctor, became the catalyst for his own spiritual awakening and relationship with God.[1]

Father Bezmenov sees beyond Yuri's disappointment and anger. He gently tells him that God has kept him alive and brought him out of prison for a reason; that God desires a relationship imprinted in his life, not only on his chest. He offers Yuri food and

---

1. Solzhenitsyn, *Gulag Archipelago*, 611–15.

clothing and a place to stay. In a scene like Rublev's famous icon of the Holy Trinity ("The Hospitality of Abraham"), Father Bezmenov's expression of generous hospitality invites Yuri into God's circle of love.[2]

God does not shun or grow impatient with rough characters like Yuri, but warmly opens his arms to embrace them in loving hospitality. God is building his kingdom with the rough misshapen "stones that the builders rejected"—people like Yuri who need someone they can totally trust and who loves them in spite of everything and more deeply than they know.

GOD IS RELATIONAL

The story of God's relationship with the children of Israel is one of unending love. The Scripture records the descendants of Jacob (Israel) falling into captivity and slavery under the rule of Egyptian pharaohs. They are considered among the least significant of all people and not even a real nation. But God sees their suffering and humiliation, mercifully delivering them from slavery to establish them as his holy people, a witness of his love to the nations. Despite God's loving-kindness and mercy toward them, the people continue in willfulness, obstinacy, and unfaithfulness. Again and again, from one generation to another, God's love for them never wanes as he keeps rescuing and restoring them from troubles of their own making. His love for them despite their stubborn waywardness is an awesome story.

Even though God rescues and delivers them from defeat and captivity to other nations, the children of Israel continually betray God's love for them. Yet God persists in drawing them back into His embrace. Philip Yancey describes the Old Testament accounts

2. Andrei Rublev (1360–1430) painted the icon of the Holy Trinity, which is also known as "The Hospitality of Abraham." The painting depicts three figures seated in harmony around a table enjoying the hospitality offered to three strangers by Abraham and Sarah, who are implied in the background. The icon is held at Trinity Monastery of Saint Sergius, located in Sergiyev Posad, about thirty-five miles from Moscow.

of God's persistent love in the face of Israel's unfaithfulness as the story of "God, a jilted lover."[3] Time and again the people turn their backs on God to worship other gods, yet God keeps "wooing" them back into relationship with himself. The Old Testament story of Hosea and his unfaithful wife, Gomer, is a metaphor of God's ever-loving relationship with Israel despite their repetitive unfaithfulness, infidelity, and idolatry. God's love for the disobedient children of Israel who prostitute themselves to the idols of foreign gods goes deeper than their own skin-deep allegiance to him.

Many imprisoned and marginalized people like Eddie and Yuri have no inkling or expectation of God's endless love for them. They have been repeatedly hurt and disappointed in human relationships and have extraordinarily little trust or hope in others. Because of the way people have treated him all his life, Eddie is suffocating under a sense of worthlessness and unworthiness. He knows that he is a failure and therefore unlovable. Deep down he hungers for love and acceptance that no one so far has shown him. Yuri believes there is a God but has not experienced God. He needs a friend he can trust, someone like Father Bezmenov to care enough for him to offer hospitality and to walk with him in friendship. That is what a relationship with God looks like.

It is exceedingly difficult for people who do not have relationships that hold up through their failures and disappointments to trust that God loves them no matter what. God may not get them out of trouble or deliver them from the consequences of their misdeeds, but he will not shun them the way most people do. He will be right there with them in the humiliation of guilt, judgment, and imprisonment. Yuri and Eddie have been judged and rejected for what they have done and that colors how people tend to see them for what and who they are. But God loves them and welcomes them into the loving circle of relationship with him, no matter what.

In the beginning God created the heavens and the earth. The apex of his creation was human life, persons made in his own image. From creation onwards, Scripture portrays God as being ever

3. Yancey and Quinn, *Meet the Bible*, 282.

relational, reaching out to the people of his creation who become disobedient and turn their backs on him; reaching out in love to troublemakers and those who have fallen into trouble of their own making.

Here are just a few troublemaker recipients to illustrate the point . . .

God is described in personal terms as being the God of Abraham, Isaac, and Jacob. He thereby defines himself forever as being in relationship with flawed humans. When Abraham consorts with Hagar, Sarah's maidservant, she subsequently bears a son, Ishmael. Abraham the rejects her and Ishmael, sending them into dangerous and painful exile. Yet God does not reject Abraham as Abraham rejected Hagar, even though it was Abraham who sinned against her. God responds mercifully to Abraham and graciously sustains and blesses Hagar and Ishmael in their distress.

Amid Job's personal suffering and ruin God remains with him and sustains him through all the calamity, including Job's deep doubt and questioning of God's intentions. Why do bad things happen to good people? Job's friends challenge him, and when they abandon him to his misery, God remains with him, ultimately restoring Job to a position far beyond anything he had known.

During their slavery and oppression in Egypt, God hears the groaning of the Israelites and appoints Moses, a murderer living in desert exile, to lead the people into freedom. When Moses becomes impatient and when the people grumble, complain, and disobey, God nevertheless provides for them because he loves them.

The Psalms reveal a remarkably close and complex relationship between King David and God. Through success and failure, good times as well as hard times, through obedience and disobedience, God does not give up on David. Even in the shadow of David's sordid affair with Bathsheba and the conspiracy to have her husband Uriah killed, God does not withdraw his love from David.

Throughout the Old Testament God is portrayed as conversing with marginalized and strange people like Isaiah, Jeremiah, Ezekiel, Daniel, and Jonah. When Jonah balks at taking God's message of hope and salvation to the sin city of Nineveh, God persists and speaks to Jonah even in the belly of a whale, to bring the Ninevites into relationship with himself because he loves them as much as he loves Jonah.

Of course, anyone reading Exodus and Deuteronomy as well as other accounts in the Old Testament can get the impression that God is a strict legalist who loves obedient and responsive people, while wreaking vengeance on people who are disobedient. Indeed, there are stories that seem to portray God as a merciless judge. However, the overwhelming and much fuller picture of God is that he is loving, merciful, patient, and forgiving in relation to disobedient people.

There is a place for judgment and punishment, but God's primary modus operandi is love. He is not, as some imagine, a cosmic policeman who acts primarily to reward the faithful and punish the disobedient. Most Christians would not describe God like that, but their response and attitude toward people like Yuri and Eddie conveys the impression that God judges and distances himself from wrongdoers. After all, doesn't God have zero tolerance for sin? Will he not ultimately judge all people by rewarding believers for doing the right thing, and punishing unbelievers, criminals, and all who do wrong and hurtful things?

GOD IS HOLY

The clear message of Scripture is that God, in fact, is holy and has zero tolerance for sin. In Leviticus, nearly eighty references to the holiness of God paint a clear distinction between God and sinful human beings, who are continually called to turn away from their sin toward God. "For I am the Lord who brought you up out of the land of Egypt to be your God. You shall therefore be holy, for I am holy."[4]

In considering God's holiness, the psalmist asks two rhetorical questions: "Who may ascend the hill of the Lord? Who may stand in his holy place? He who has clean hands and a pure heart,

---

4. Leviticus 11:45.

who does not lift up his soul to an idol or swear by what is false."[5] Peter, in a letter to the early church, applies this as a principle for holy and obedient living: "As obedient children, do not conform to the evil desires you had when you lived in ignorance. But just as he who called you is holy, so be holy in all you do; for it is written: 'Be holy, because I am holy.'"[6]

In one of the most memorable expressions of God's holiness, the prophet Isaiah has a vision of God's holiness that leaves him feeling totally unclean and inadequate in relation to God. "Holy, holy, holy is the Lord Almighty; the whole earth is full of his glory" . . . "'Woe to me!' I cried. 'For I am a man of unclean lips, and I live among a people of unclean lips, and my eyes have seen the King, the Lord Almighty.'"[7]

However, God's holiness is not unmitigated separation between himself and impure humanity. The prophet Habbakuk addresses the apparent disconnect between God's holiness and evil in the world. "Your eyes are too pure to look on evil; you cannot tolerate wrongdoing. Why then do you tolerate the treacherous? Why are you silent while the wicked swallow up those more righteous than themselves?"[8] Habbakuk knows that God is holy and yet in recognizing the reality of evil and treachery in the world he trusts that God will not abandon humanity but will act to establish righteousness and eradicate evil forever.

Job grappled mightily with the conundrum of a holy and all-powerful God who seems to allow an innocent man like himself to suffer while wicked persons flourish and go unpunished.

> How then can I dispute with him?
> How can I find words to argue with him?
> Though I were innocent, I could not answer him;
> I could only plead with my Judge for mercy.
> Even if I summoned him and he responded,
> I do not believe he would give me a hearing.

5. Psalm 24:3–4.
6. 1 Peter 1:16.
7. Isaiah 63:5.
8. Habbakuk 1:13.

He would crush me with a storm
    and multiply my wounds for no reason.
He would not let me catch my breath
    but would overwhelm me with misery.
If it is a matter of strength, he is mighty!
    And if it is a matter of justice, who can challenge him?
Even if I were innocent, my mouth would condemn me;
    if I were blameless, it would pronounce me guilty.
"Although I am blameless,
    I have no concern for myself;
    I despise my own life.
It is all the same; that is why I say,
    "He destroys both the blameless and the wicked."
When a scourge brings sudden death,
    he mocks the despair of the innocent.
When a land falls into the hands of the wicked,
    he blindfolds its judges.
If it is not he, then who is it?[9]

So, if God is holy and God is all-powerful, how does that impinge on his relation to humanity? At one level holiness means that God is uniquely pure, without rival or competition, peerless. God identifies himself to Moses as "I am who I am."[10] This enigmatic declaration can be variously translated as "I will become what I choose to become," "I am what I am," "I will be what I will be," "I create what(ever) I create," or "I am the Existing One."[11] When Scripture calls God holy it means that God is completely beyond humanness and impurity. The notion of God's absolute moral purity is just one aspect of being holy. In biblical usage the primary meaning of *holy* means "separate" and is derived from a word meaning to cut or to divide, denoting a clear distinction between what is holy and everything else. To say that God hates sin and has no tolerance for evil implies a definitive distinction between God and everything sinful and evil.

---

9. Job 9:14–24.

10. Exodus 3:14.

11. Freedman et al., eds., *Eerdmans Dictionary of the Bible*, 624.

The expression "God hates sin but loves the sinner" is sometimes used to affirm the dignity and worth of persons despite their wrongful actions, as a way of dealing with the conundrum between God's love for humanity and the fact that God does not "tolerate" sin.

The holiness of God is transcendent, beyond anything that can be apprehended or attained through human experience in the material universe. Holiness differentiates all that is God from all that is human. Commonly we think of God's being holy as one among other attributes of God, such as God knows everything (omniscience), God is everywhere present (omnipresence), God is all powerful (omnipotence). God is love, God is just, God is merciful and gracious, etc. All of these are true. However, holiness is not just another of those attributes. Holiness encompasses all God's attributes and thus God's love is holy, God's justice (and God's judgment) is holy, God's mercy is holy, and so forth. Every characteristic of God is incomparable to and differentiated from human qualities of the same name because God's characteristics are holy and pure, uncompromised and untainted by evil.

This understanding of God's holiness is important because it means that we cannot define God's love, justice, or mercy based on our unholy human sensibilities, experience, and expectations. Even our understanding of God's holy love is limited, colored by our own experiences, ideas, reasoning, and expectations of love. God's love is always above and beyond human love and cannot be contained within any paradigm of human love.

God's love is so totally different from any human love that Eddie and Yuri have ever known that it is virtually impossible for them to understand how deeply, unequivocally, and endlessly God loves them. And it is also hard for us to believe that a holy God totally and completely embraces criminals and the most reprehensible of offenders with love.

GOD IS LOVE

From the beginning, love has been the most definitive and predominant characteristic of God's relationship with humanity. Adam and Eve had everything given to them with only one thing forbidden. As soon as the opportunity presented itself, they turned away from God and did that one thing. They suffered the consequences of disobedience, but God still loved and cared for them, even providing garments to cover their sense of naked shame. When their son Cain murdered his brother Abel, he was banished from the land, but God still loved and protected him.

As the human story continues, evil mars the relationship between God and humanity. Time and again God mercifully rescues humanity through people like Noah, Abraham, Isaac, and Jacob. These are not perfect people, but God loves them even when they fail and disobey. God's love for Abraham's descendants through their frequent idolatry is a love story like no other. God's love undergirds them with compassion and forgiveness. "The LORD, the LORD, the compassionate and gracious God, slow to anger, abounding in love and faithfulness, maintaining love to thousands, and forgiving wickedness, rebellion and sin."[12]

God's endless love perseveres and endures amidst human disobedience and the consequences of their own making—promises deferred, wilderness exile, battles lost, and foreign captivity. God even makes his presence and love for them visible through covenant, and tabernacle and temple worship: "I will make an everlasting covenant with them: I will never stop doing good to them, and I will inspire them to fear me, so that they will never turn away from me. I will rejoice in doing them good and will assuredly plant them in this land with all my heart and soul."[13]

Through prophets, priests, and poets like David, God continually offers people love and help; and when they turn to him, he delivers them from their enemies, restores their land, and gives them yet another chance: "Rend your heart and not your garments.

12. Exodus 34:6–7.
13. Jeremiah 32:40–41.

Return to the LORD your God, for he is gracious and compassionate, slow to anger and abounding in love, and he relents from sending calamity. Who knows? He may turn and have pity and leave behind a blessing . . ."[14] Within this larger story are many compelling stories of God loving individuals in trouble, whether because of their own misdeeds or at the hands of others. The biblical story portrays God's unfailing, unending love.

When God's patient, persistent love is unrequited and the people are in captivity again, he promises to redeem and restore them because they are still precious to him (Isaiah 43). Then, in Jesus of Nazareth, God comes into their midst as one of them to show them the depth and extent of his love for them—love that ultimately takes the consequences of (their) sin upon himself so they can be redeemed and restored into relationship with himself and each other.

Of course, the Scripture also recounts times when God is angered by the disobedience of people, when he punishes and allows them to suffer the consequence of their sin. But God's punishment is ever in the context and constraints of his holy love. God's love is the "big picture" within which God acts, even if it is to punish wrongdoing and evil.

In his letter to a young church, Paul reminds the followers of Jesus in Corinth of God's holy love, and the qualities of love that should characterize their love for others. He draws no circle around such love, no boundaries as to who is to be included or excluded from the loving embrace of God's kingdom. "Love is patient, love is kind. It does not envy, it does not boast, it is not proud. It does not dishonor others, it is not self-seeking, it is not easily angered, it keeps no record of wrongs. Love does not delight in evil but rejoices with the truth. It always protects, always trusts, always hopes, always perseveres. Love never fails."[15]

When Fr. Bezmenov humbly extends hospitality to a belligerent Yuri, he expects nothing in return. It is a simple, generous expression of God's love for a broken man, a stone who the builders

14. Joel 2:12–14.
15. 1 Corinthians 13:4–7.

of society rejected. He knows that God desires a relationship with Yuri that is more than skin deep. He also understands that it is one thing to tell Yuri about God's love, and it is quite another to love Yuri as God loves him.

God's love is without boundary. It is never superficial and always more than skin deep.

CHAPTER 4

The Justice of God

Beyond Fair Judgment

EDDIE'S DEEPEST YEARNING IS to get out from under the judgment of being a failure and to be loved and valued as a human being regardless of his inability to help himself. As a young man the only love he has known is love from which he is excluded because he is not good enough. He has been judged by the people around him and by the law; by every measure he deserves imprisonment. Eddie knows that, and yet his heart cries out for someone to accept and care for him despite his crimes and failure.

Yuri demands to be judged fairly. If God really loves him, he would surely have done something to get him out of his imprisonment for something that was not his fault. Like him, most people think God's love and justice means mercy for victims of wrongdoing and injustice on the one hand, and judgment and punishment for those who commit evil and perpetrate injustice on the other hand. While this seems to be fair at the level of common sense, Scripture identifies God both as the judge of all people and the one who loves all of humanity without any precondition. God does not apportion his love to those who are deserving and withhold love from those who are undeserving. The psalmist depicts God's love as utterly faithful. Justice and righteousness are the foundation of his throne and issue forth in love and faithfulness.

"Righteousness and justice are the foundation of your throne; love and faithfulness go before you."[1] Isaiah and the prophets also proclaim the heart of God's justice as interconnected with grace and compassion in response to his people, though they are disobedient and in trouble: "the LORD longs to be gracious to you; therefore, he will rise up to show you compassion. For the LORD is a God of justice."[2]

DEFINING JUSTICE

The idea of justice is loaded with complex and often competing expectations, implications, and meanings. Consider the application of justice in addressing wrongs and inequities in just four areas of life.

- "Distributive justice"—concerning the disparity of economic opportunity and well-being between groups of people in a society and in the world.

- "Global justice"—concerning the abuse of military, economic, and political power by nations and corporations to the detriment of other nations and peoples.

- "Social justice"—the protection and exercise of human rights and responsibilities for the well-being and flourishing of all people regardless of race, culture, gender identity, age, religion, creed, political persuasion, etc.

- "Criminal justice"—maintaining law and order in society through fair and effective law enforcement, honest investigation of offenses, fair prosecution and trial of accused offenders, the humane punishment of those found guilty, and the protection and support of victims.

The application of justice in these areas and beyond has relevance to virtually every aspect of our lives and is built on a sense

1. Psalm 89:14.
2. Isaiah 30:18.

of virtue, rectitude, and fairness as measurements or standards by which actions are judged to be right or wrong. Aristotle suggests that justice as a virtue implies relationality and morality, in that justice involves a relationship between people; justice is what people owe to each other and expect from one another. Similarly, while love and mercy are virtues that also exist in the relational space between people, they are often seen as being distinct or separate from justice. Justice is typically relegated to the act of passing fair and equitable judgment on a person's behavior or actions and thus distancing that person from others.

Typically, we think that justice is served when persons are judged and treated as their wrongful actions deserve, and that such judgment is made without preference for or prejudice against those involved. But is this really tantamount to justice? What does justice really look like when justice is done—for offenders, for victims, for the community? When Scripture describes God as being just, what does that mean in terms of God also being merciful and loving toward all people, victims and offenders alike?

JUSTICE AND JUDGMENT

Although the delivery of justice is ideally based on impartial, fair, and right judgment, the goal of justice is not fulfilled in right judgment, whether through acquittal or punishment. Justice is ultimately accomplished when the wrongdoing and the damage caused by wrongdoing is put right (more about this in chapter 7). Yet without standards of what is just and right as the basis for upholding good and censuring what is wrong, society would end up becoming completely disordered and anarchic.

Sanctions against evil, punishment as a deterrent and consequence for wrongdoing, are necessary for maintaining the social order and keeping peace among people. However, justice that stops at sanctions and punishment is incomplete, for it neither rights the wrong that has been committed nor remedies the physical, social, emotional, and spiritual harms caused by wrongdoing. The following examples may help to illustrate the difference between judgment and justice, even when judgment is considered to be fair, proportionate, and equitable . . .

Andrew's prison sentence is considered fair. He could have been sentenced to much more than ten years in prison given the severity of his crime. Nevertheless, by the time he completes his ten years behind bars he has lost his partner, family, friends, as well as his home and livelihood and place in the community. Imprisonment was punishment enough, but the consequence of having served ten years in prison, separated from the community, is another sort of punishment. When he returns to the community he is marked as an ex-con, a flawed character, a person not to be trusted. Imprisonment has not changed his life for the better and has done nothing by way of compensating the victims of his crime for their loss and hurt. Even though Andrew's conviction and imprisonment has given them a small measure of satisfaction, the damage caused by Andrew's crime has left them with painful emotional scars and economic loss. Within a year of his release from prison, Andrew finds himself homeless and unemployed. He ends up falling in with ex-cons like himself and it isn't long before he is back in prison for dealing drugs just to survive.

Ruth is simply doing a favor for her new boyfriend when she checks his luggage along with her own at the airport. She is excited about their plans for an exotic holiday together. During the stopover for a connecting flight in Thailand, inspectors discover a large quantity of illegal drugs in her boyfriend's luggage. Unaware of the contents of his luggage, Ruth is shocked to suddenly find herself surrounded by police, handcuffed, and charged with international drug smuggling. Somehow, her new boyfriend disappears, and she never sees him again. Because she checked his luggage in under her name, she is left "holding the bag." Ruth's pleas of innocence do not stand up to prosecution, her defense is weak, and she is subsequently judged guilty by the judge and sentenced to twenty years in a Thai prison for women. As far as the police and prosecutors are concerned, justice is being served. Ruth should have known better, but she was naïve and in love with her boyfriend. She was blind to the fact that he was simply using her to courier drugs. Drug trafficking is a serious crime in which Ruth was an unwittingly accomplice. While her conviction and imprisonment might deter other potential offenders, the judgment against her does nothing to address the reality of her own victimization.

"The charges are unfair, trumped up against me. Everything I did was completely legal," declares Phil. He is dressed in an orange prison jumpsuit, his legs secured in iron shackles. He looks miserable. Phil has always been a dreamer and a schemer, but he is not a violent man. When the possibility of making a lot of money through a novel financial scheme was presented to him, he bought into the opportunity with the same passion he pursued every project. This was his best chance to make it big! Unknown to Phil, the proposed scheme was a complex police sting operation—he had no idea that there was anything wrong with the proposal. Now he feels that the justice system has unfairly manipulated him and entrapped him. Besides Phil, there are others involved but they have struck plea bargains and will end up paying fines, not serving time. Phil probably should have known better than to fall for a scheme that was too good to be true. If he is guilty of anything it is greed. There are no victims, there is no loss of money, only the gullibility of a man falling for a scheme that constituted a "conspiracy to defraud." There are situations when justice is perverted under the guise of pursuing justice.

"This is not justice," screams Maria as her day in a Mexican district court is postponed for the fifth time in as many months. "I have no money for a lawyer," she shouts over the judge's warning, "and now I have been evicted from my house! My daughter and house are all I have; your justice is a filthy lie!" The judge bangs his gavel down with a stern reprimand, "I have warned you before, and now you will serve ten days in jail for contempt. The court will appoint a public defender, and for now, your daughter can be placed in the care of relatives." The circumstances of Maria's case involve theft from her employer, who had loaned her a small amount of money for rent. She was not making enough money from her work to make repayment. When opportunities came she took small amounts of cash from the shop where she worked. Maria is a poor, widowed, and uneducated laborer. Even though her employer is wealthy, he does not pay his workers a living wage. Like so many others, Maria has been taking a little here and a little there to be able to make monthly rent payments on her tiny flat and have money to clothe and feed her young daughter. What she has done is wrong and that is the only consideration of the court. When she finally has her day in court, judgment is pronounced, and she is sentenced to prison. There is so much wrong in the circumstances contributing to her situation that was not even considered by the judge.

Joshua watches in helpless, desperate anguish as a gang of Rwandan Hutu militants savagely rape and skin his young niece alive, then dump her in a field to die. There is no one to intervene. Inhumanity and injustice ravage the country with impunity. After one hundred days more than eight hundred thousand massacred Rwandans lie dead in city streets, float on muddy rivers, rot in abandoned homes, and rest lifelessly in churches where victims have sought shelter from the killers. In the aftermath of genocide there is not enough space in prisons and makeshift stockades to hold the participants in the genocide. Next to nothing remains of the justice system. There are few judges or lawyers left in the country and the rule of law has literally been destroyed. In any case, what means or measure of justice can ever undo or compensate for the brutal savagery that has destroyed the lives, property, and livelihood of Rwandan victims and survivors? "The normal justice process, if we had one, could never begin to address the vast scope of the horrendous crimes that were committed," states President Kagama soon after order is restored by his new government. "What can we possibly do with all our prisoners, and all the victims? It will take forever to process every case!"

How can justice ever repair the damage of so great an evil as genocide? There are crimes and evil so extensive and deep that they are impossible to deal with, humanly speaking, and so we weep in solidarity with those who have suffered, and we weep in agony and impotence to know how justice can be done or what justice even means. Judgment and punishment can never repay the loss and assuage the suffering of so many at the hands of their fellow Rwandans.

CRYING FOR JUSTICE

Victims and offenders alike yearn for justice, justice that understands their circumstances and feels their pain. The people in the preceding stories are real people who are suffering not only the consequences of crime and violence—they are also suffering from the lack of justice.

Like them, we also cry out for justice when we suffer the consequences of our own wrongdoing and wrongs committed against us.

- When we have done something that wrongs another person and much as we regret it, we cannot undo the damage and hurt we have caused.

- When we witness an act of injustice or wrongdoing against another person and are powerless to intervene.

- When a judgment of wrongdoing against someone who has harmed us does not address the damage done, restore our sense of well being, or make things right.

- When the punishment of an offender results in collateral damage to their families and their future, and is considered "case closed" without providing satisfaction to victims and the community.

Since ancient times, the cry for justice that makes things right has been universal. This hunger for justice cannot be fully satisfied simply by judging and punishing those who do wrong. Victims of discrimination, violence, abuse of power, deception, theft, mistreatment, and all manner of wrongdoing cry out not only for punishment but for someone to undo the wrong and make things right. Yet, there seems to be no satisfactory way of doing justice that sets things right for all, for victims and offenders alike. Usually, the best that victims can expect is for offenders to be punished. But even the satisfaction of seeing their offenders punished does nothing to repair the damage, reclaim the loss, or restore the well-being of the victim.

The prophet Amos laments the pervasive wrongdoing of his people. Through their actions and ways of living the poor are exploited, the rights and dignity of the vulnerable are trampled, and those in power profiteer through bribery and extortion, twisting truth, and perverting the course of justice. Beneath the opulent veneer of their well-being, their festivals and feasts, are people marginalized and victimized at the expense of others. Amos gives voice to their thirst for justice: "Let justice roll down like waters, and righteousness like an ever-flowing stream."[3]

Zechariah, one of the last of the Old Testament prophets, acknowledges the historic wickedness (injustice) and unfaithfulness (idolatry) of his people who have repeatedly and chronically betrayed God's relationship with them, by not loving him with all their heart, soul, and might and by not loving their neighbors as themselves. Even though God has been very patient with them, he has allowed them to reap the consequences of their wrongdoing. They have fallen into captivity, their land has been overtaken by foreign powers, their temple destroyed, and the people subjected to exile and servitude. However, God has not simply given them over to this punishment. He continues to reach out to them in compassion and love, offering forgiveness, help, and restoration.

Wickedness and infidelity have not negated God's overarching love and grace. There is hope for his people amid punishment and exile. Zechariah powerfully reminds the people that God's relationship with them does not end with judgment and punishment but with hope and restoration: "As for you, because of the blood of my covenant with you, I will free your prisoners from the waterless pit. Return to your fortress, you prisoners of hope; even now I announce that I will restore twice as much to you."[4]

3. Amos 5:24.
4. Zechariah 9:11–12.

JUSTICE AND MERCY

It is impossible to separate the punishment of criminal offenders from the need for justice; it is impossible to equate the punishment of criminal offenders with justice.

Offenders who have been found guilty of serious crimes are typically sentenced to serve time in prison as punishment. They are getting what they deserve for their offenses. Caring for the imprisoned is considered a work of mercy, mercy for the undeserving. Judgment and punishment do not preclude mercy but make mercy possible, occasion the need for mercy. Offenders may deserve punishment, but they also need mercy and they need grace. Judgment and mercy are neither disconnected or disparate actions of God. Both judgment and mercy are expressions of God's love, and are part of God's justice.

God's relationship with the children of Israel shows that his judgment and mercy are not polarized opposites but interwoven in the fabric of justice. Like other prophets, Micah recounts the overarching graciousness of God even as the people transgress his law and turn their backs on relationship with him. Throughout their history of repeated unfaithfulness God remains faithful and persists in drawing them back into relationship. In his relationship with them God also reveals what he expects of them: "He has shown you, O mortal, what is good. And what does the LORD require of you? To act justly and to love mercy and to walk humbly with your God."[5]

In a similar vein, the psalmist reflects on the experience of God's grace as the people are being punished for wrongdoing.

5. Micah 6:8. Some translations express this more poignantly than the NIV. The ESV states, "He has told you, O man, what is good; and what does the Lord require of you but to do justice, and to love kindness, and to walk humbly with your God?" The CEV states, "The Lord God has told us what is right and what he demands: "See that justice is done, let mercy be your first concern, and humbly obey your God." The NRSV states, "He has told you, O mortal, what is good; and what does the Lord require of you but to do justice, and to love kindness, and to walk humbly with your God?"

Punishment is not the end of justice, but by God's overarching love, redemption and restoration come through his grace and mercy.

> Some sat in darkness, in utter darkness,
>   prisoners suffering in iron chains,
> because they rebelled against God's commands
>   and despised the plans of the Most High.
> So he subjected them to bitter labor;
>   they stumbled, and there was no one to help.
> Then they cried to the LORD in their trouble,
>   and he saved them from their distress.
> He brought them out of darkness, the utter darkness,
>   and broke away their chains.
> Let them give thanks to the LORD for his unfailing love
>   and his wonderful deeds for mankind,
> for he breaks down gates of bronze
>   and cuts through bars of iron.[6]

GOD'S JUSTICE IS HOLY

God is holy, and in the same way that God's love is holy so also is God's justice. God's love cannot be understood or contained in terms of human qualities of love; neither can God's justice be contained or understood in terms of human concepts of justice.

As with love, God's justice is expressed in relationship with people. The scriptural sense of justice is not an abstract ideal or legal formulation but expressed interpersonally, relationally. The two Hebrew words commonly translated as justice are *tzedek* and *mishpat*, the full meanings of which are not easily captured. Sometimes, *tzedek* is translated into English as "justice" and at other times as "righteousness," depending on the context. While both justice and righteousness are inherent in the Hebrew meaning of *tzedek,* the word embodies a richer meaning than is conveyed by justice and righteousness. *Tzedek* embodies compassion, relationality, making things right, restoring wholeness, and making peace. It means much more than fair legal judgment or right adjudication.

---

6. Psalm 107:10–16.

The compassionate and relational connotation of *tzedek* embodies the Hebrew notion of *shalom*, which means peace in the sense of well-being and wholeness as well as the absence of conflict. The rich synergy of *tzedek* and *shalom* is captured poetically by the psalmist in declaring "love and faithfulness meet together; righteousness and peace kiss each other."[7] Justice and righteousness embody peace that is experienced in the well-being and harmony of community relationships. Peace (*shalom*) is possible only through harmony between people, relationships that express justice and righteousness (*tzedek*).

The other Hebrew word, *mishpat*, which is also translated as "justice," implies fair laws and fair judgment associated with right behavior for the common good or well-being of the community. While the Old Testament Scriptures present a picture of God's justice in which offenders come under judgment for wrongdoing and are punished, it also upholds those who are victimized and exploited. Justice is advanced through right judgment and punishment of offenders and the rescue/restoration of victims to the end that relationships are put right, and the well-being of the community is restored. God instructs his people to pursue this kind of justice in order to flourish in the land he is giving them: "Justice, justice you shall pursue, so that you may thrive and occupy the land that the Lord your God is giving you."[8]

God's justice is realized in judgment interwoven with love, compassion, and salvation. Some scholars refer to this as God's saving justice, or God's merciful justice. It is justice accomplished when wrongs have been made right through restoring, healing, and transforming relationships damaged by evil and wrongdoing. Quite literally, the good news (the gospel) is that God's justice is more than the fair execution of judgment and punishment against offenders. God's overarching purpose is to save humanity from sin and evil by restoring all things—individuals, societies, nations, nature.

7. Psalm 85:10.
8. Deuteronomy 16:20.

JUSTICE FOR ALL

Compared to God's way of justice, what we typically call justice is relationally toxic and does not lead to restoration and peace (it does not resolve the hurt or damage—and generally culminates in punishment without repair, reform, restoration, or reconciliation). While criminal and civil justice are the responsibility of governments, this does not mean individuals, communities, and the church do not have a vital role to play in pursuing justice in ways that reflect God's heart for justice that does bring about restoration, healing, reconciliation, and peace. There are many opportunities for engaging with offenders, victims, and families as a compassionate expression of God's redemptive love and mercy. These range from speaking out against unfair judgment and corrupt justice systems that are inequitable; upholding the cause of people who are oppressed and exploited; caring for the victims of crime; reaching out to offenders with hope and love; supporting the families of imprisoned offenders; advocating for measures of doing justice that facilitate restoration and reconciliation. It is in pursuing justice beyond judgment and punishment that we participate with God in his redemption of the world.

While our normal way of seeking justice in society tends to focus on judgment and punishment, it opens opportunities for expressing the compassion, love, and mercy by which God draws both offenders and victims to himself. God is love. God is just. God's judgment and mercy are interwoven to the end of restoring community peace and well-being, healing broken relationships, and setting things right for those who suffer under the yokes of exploitation, injustice, and inequity.

Isaiah prophetically paints a picture of God's justice being fully accomplished through the "Servant of the Lord" who embodies God's redemptive love and mercy.

> Here is my servant, whom I uphold,
>   my chosen one in whom I delight;
> I will put my Spirit on him,
>   and he will bring justice to the nations.

He will not shout or cry out,
    or raise his voice in the streets.
A bruised reed he will not break,
    and a smoldering wick he will not snuff out.
In faithfulness he will bring forth justice;
he will not falter or be discouraged
till he establishes justice on earth.[9]

9. Isaiah 42:1-4.

CHAPTER 5

The Mercy of God

Beyond Second Chances

WHEN EXPECTATIONS FOR JUSTICE are not met by courts of justice and when judgment and punishment seem too lenient, there is a sense in which justice has not been served. It is not uncommon for people to seek revenge for wrongdoing through vigilante justice, to take matters into their own hands.

This happened in a community that was fed up with Jacob, a thief who snatched purses and jewelry from unsuspecting tourists and would not stop stealing from shops and vendors during their peak business hours. More than just being a nuisance, his brash behavior was threatening the tourist trade, as well as eating into business profits. Some people saw Jacob, who was homeless, as simply being a sick man who needed psychological treatment. Others were so angered by his brazen purse-snatching and thievery that they determined to put an end to it, to deliver the justice that authorities seemed unwilling or unable to.

The opportunity came when Jacob was caught in the act of wresting a woman's handbag from her shoulder. Before he could make a run for it, an angry mob of shopkeepers and bystanders surrounded him. What they did next amounted to the "wild justice" of revenge. Jacob was "necklaced"'—a rubber car tire was forced around his shoulders, filled with petrol, and set on fire.

Jacob's fiery, gruesome death was applauded by the crowd of spectators and sent a message to other thieves. There would be no more tolerance for street thieves in Nairobi.

Necklacing, lynching, shooting, beating, and other forms of retaliation seem to satisfy our human instinct for revenge against drug lords, sexual predators, fraudsters, mobsters, and marauders who prey on vulnerable victims. Instances of public and private revenge give expression to the instinctive vocabulary of human justice. While blatant acts of revenge are usually not condoned, acts of revenge differ only in degree from verbal demands for tougher sentencing and harsher prison conditions when the judgments of the court seem too lenient and soft.

PUNISHMENT DESERVED

Jacob had a long criminal record. He had been arrested numerous times prior to his death and had served several prison terms. Prison did nothing to change his behavior and it was apparent to the people that Jacob deserved harsher punishment. Mercy was out of the question, even though he was homeless and poor. Fueled by a rash of similar crimes in the community, there was growing public appetite for tough justice. So, when Jacob was caught and necklaced at the hands of angry shopkeepers, most people felt that he got exactly the justice he deserved.

There was no question of Jacob deserving another chance. He had used up his second chances. He was a repeat offender and had been caught red-handed. Possibly, if this had been his first offense, or if he had been young and orphaned, or if he was physically disabled or mentally challenged—perhaps then he would have been seen as someone deserving mercy, or at least have been given another chance.

The fact is that mercy is not mercy if it is something a person deserves. Mercy, by definition, is always undeserved. Mercy can be defined as withholding the punishment that judgment demands. Justice and mercy are typically thought of as being opposites. Justice is understood as a right judgment that results in due consequences, the punishment of the offender. However, mercy means that the punishment an offender rightly deserves is cancelled. Justice and mercy exist in a tension that St. Thomas Aquinas observes as being a necessary relationship. He postulated that mercy without justice is the mother of dissolution, whereas justice without mercy is cruelty. For Aquinas, the overarching ethic of love demands that justice be done with mercy and that mercy not undermine the standards of justice.

THE HEART OF MERCY

Mercy is derived from the Latin word *misericordia,* which conveys the image of a sorrowful or compassionate heart. *Misericordia* is the combination of two words: *misereri,* meaning to have pity on or feel compassion for someone; and *cordis,* meaning "of the heart." The root idea of mercy is that of showing compassion to someone from the inmost depth (or heart) of ones' being. Mercy is inherently the kindly consideration of one person toward another without being prejudiced by what the recipient deserves.

In the Old Testament, the most frequently used Hebrew word for mercy is *chesed,* meaning loving-kindness or a steadfast love that is persistent and freely given. *Chesed* occurs nearly 250 times in the Old Testament, with about half of those occurrences being in the Psalms. God expects his people to be merciful toward one another because God is merciful toward them, in response to their wrongdoing and disobedience. God is merciful because of his steadfast love for them. The Scriptures declare God's covenant with his people as being one of mercy (*chesed*) despite their repeated rebelliousness.

> Many times he delivered them,
>   but they were bent on rebellion
>   and they wasted away in their sin.
> Yet he took note of their distress
>   when he heard their cry;
> for their sake he remembered his covenant
>   and out of his great love he relented.

He caused all who held them captive
to show them mercy.[1]

A Hebrew word frequently used in tandem with *chesed* is *rachamim*. *Rachamim* is an emotionally laden word that conveys an image like that of the unbounded passionate love of a mother for her child. This word is used by Isaiah in describing the depth of God's "maternal" love for his people: "Can a mother forget the baby at her breast and have no compassion (*rachamim*) on the child she has borne? Though she may forget, I will not forget you!"[2]

Rachamim also describes the depth of Joseph's response to his brothers during their reunion in Egypt, even though they had disowned him and sold him as a slave to the Egyptians: "Deeply moved (*rachamim*) at the sight of his brother, Joseph hurried out and looked for a place to weep. He went into his private room and wept there."[3]

The story is told of a frightened young soldier who, during the Napoleonic Wars, deserted his post and duty as sentry. Since this was the second time he had deserted his duty, he was charged with treason, summarily convicted, and sentenced to death by the military tribunal. When news reached his mother, she was overwrought with love and compassion for her son. In desperation she appealed directly to Napoleon. Falling to her knees before him, she pleaded with him to spare the life of her son.

"I am not asking you for justice, I am begging you for mercy. He is my only son!"

"Your son does not deserve mercy!" countered Napoleon.

Undeterred by his rebuke and moved only by love for her son, the weeping mother persisted, "But sir, it would not be mercy if he deserved it, I am begging you for mercy—please have mercy!"

Touched by the mother's deep compassion and love for her son, Napoleon relented and granted her request. By staying the

1. Psalm 106:43–45.
2. Isaiah 49:15.
3. Genesis 43:30.

execution that her son rightfully deserved, Napoleon granted him something he did not deserve, another chance. He got his life back.

TWO SIDES OF A COIN

Although the words *mercy* and *grace* are often used interchangeably, they are, in fact two words that describe opposite sides of the same coin. *Eleos* is the Greek word for mercy, which is an expression of pity or compassion. *Charis* is the Greek word for grace, which is an expression of loving-kindness, as in providing a benefit or gift. Mercy is an act of withholding deserved punishment or consequences, while grace is an act of granting undeserved favor or benefit. Both mercy and grace are expressions of God's steadfast love. God's steadfast love is the coin of which grace and mercy are two sides.

In steadfast love God is merciful, extending compassion and forgiveness to wrongdoers and offenders. The Hebrew Scriptures recount God's repeated acts of mercy toward his disobedient people. Even when he does not withhold the consequences of their disobedience and rebellion, he does not abandon them or write them off in judgment. God's judgment in response to disobedience is done with mercy in sight. St. Paul expresses God's mercy in the face of human disobedience like this: "Just as you who were at one time disobedient to God have now received mercy as a result of their disobedience, so they too have now become disobedient in order that they too may now receive mercy as a result of God's mercy to you. For God has bound everyone over to disobedience so that he may have mercy on them all."[4]

The story of Jonah exemplifies God's relentless mercy. When God instructs the prophet to go to Nineveh, he refuses because he thinks God should summarily judge that sinful city and destroy its inhabitants. At this Jonah is sorely disappointed and becomes very angry with God. Feeling betrayed and sorry for himself, he gets out of Nineveh and sits morosely in the shade of a tree to get

4. Romans 11:30–32.

relief from the heat of the sun. The next day the plant dies, leaving Jonah without shade from the blazing sun. At this he becomes even more furious with God. Then God points out that Jonah's perspective is all wrong, for he is more concerned about his own expectations and comfort than about the fate of the sinful Ninevite people who have mercifully been spared.

> God said to Jonah, "Is it right for you to be angry about the plant?"
>
> "It is," he said. "And I'm so angry I wish I were dead." But the LORD said, "You have been concerned about this plant, though you did not tend it or make it grow. It sprang up overnight and died overnight. And should I not have concern for the great city of Nineveh, in which there are more than a hundred and twenty thousand people who cannot tell their right hand from their left— and also many animals?"[5]

MERCY AND THE CHARACTER OF GOD

In his reflection on the message of the gospel and the character of God, Pope Francis writes, "Mercy is in reality the core of the Gospel message; it is the name of God Himself, the face with which he revealed Himself in the Old Testament and fully in Jesus Christ."[6]

The story of the Old Testament hinges on God's steadfast love expressed in mercy toward a people described in no uncertain terms as being "a rebellious and stiff-necked people."[7] Despite repeated infidelity, disobedience, and rebellion, God is merciful toward them and continually showers them with grace, from Mount Sinai through their long wilderness sojourn and into the promised land. At the very outset of their liberation from slavery God reveals himself through Moses as being "the LORD, a God of tenderness and compassion, slow to anger, rich in kindness and

---

5. Jonah 4:9–11.

6. Francis, *Name of God is Mercy*, 7.

7. Exodus 32:9–14.

faithfulness."[8] The people do nothing to deserve God's continuing loving-kindness. They grumble and complain, they turn from God to idols, and they are wilfully disobedient, seemingly at every turn. God punishes but does not abandon them. He continues to show them kindness and provide them with the sustenance they do not deserve.

Through succeeding generations God is merciful toward them, compelling them to return to him in their times of distress and disobedience. Through prophets like Joel and Isaiah God calls the people to put their hope and trust in him, for he is compassionate and merciful. "Turn to the Lord your God again, for he is all tenderness and compassion, slow to anger, rich in graciousness, and ready to relent."[9]

Perhaps no passage shows God's heart of mercy more clearly than Isaiah's proclamation of the year of the Lord's favor, the Scripture Jesus read in the synagogue at Nazareth.

> The Spirit of the Sovereign LORD is on me, because the LORD has anointed me to preach good news to the poor. He has sent me to bind up the broken-hearted, to proclaim freedom for the captives and release from darkness for the prisoners, to proclaim the year of the LORD's favor and the day of vengeance of our God, to comfort all who mourn, and provide for those who grieve in Zion—to bestow on them a crown of beauty instead of ashes, the oil of gladness instead of mourning, and a garment of praise instead of a spirit of despair. They will be called oaks of righteousness, a planting of the LORD for the display of his splendor. They will rebuild the ancient ruins and restore the places long devastated; they will renew the ruined cities that have been devastated for generations.[10]

Likewise, the psalmist repeatedly extols and celebrates God for the loving-kindness and mercy he has shown.

8. Exodus 34:6.

9. Joel 2:13.

10. Isaiah 61:1–4.

Praise the Lord! Oh, give thanks to the LORD, for He is good; For His lovingkindness is everlasting.[11] Praise the LORD, O my soul, and forget not all his benefits—who forgives all your sins and heals all your diseases, who redeems your life from the pit and crowns you with love and compassion, who satisfies your desires with good things so that your youth is renewed like the eagle's. The LORD works righteousness and justice for all the oppressed. He made known his ways to Moses, his deeds to the people of Israel: The LORD is compassionate and gracious, slow to anger, abounding in love. He will not always accuse, nor will he harbor his anger forever; he does not treat us as our sins deserve or repay us according to our iniquities.[12]

The Gospels declare the good news that God is merciful and gracious to all people, the deserving and the undeserving alike: ". . . your Father in heaven. He causes his sun to rise on the evil and the good, and sends rain on the righteous and the unrighteous."[13]

Mercy and grace are rooted in the very character of God. The Old Testament law reveals it; the wisdom literature teaches it; the prophets cry out for it; the Psalms celebrate it; and God's mercy comes to full expression in the life and teachings of Jesus Christ. C. S. Lewis considers the implications of God's mercy for human conduct: "our charity must be real and costly love, with deep feeling for the sins in spite of which we love the sinner—no mere tolerance or indulgence which parodies love . . ."[14]

THE MINISTRY OF JUSTICE AND GRACE

A bold inscription carved into the granite archway above the imposing entrance identifies the building as *Ministerio Justicia y Gracia* (Ministry of Justice and Grace). Ministry of Justice and Grace

---

11. Psalm 106:1.
12. Psalm 103:2–10.
13. Matthew 5:45.
14. Lewis, *Weight of Glory*, 45–46.

is the unusual name for Costa Rica's Department of Justice and Penitentiary Administration and seems to be a contradiction in identity and purpose.[15]

It is indeed equally difficult to grasp how justice and grace (and mercy) cohabitate in the character of God. In reading Scripture one can easily pay more attention to God judging and punishing the wicked than to his generous mercy expressed in forgiveness, restoration, and blessing toward a people who have been so disobedient and rebellious. And it is easy to overlook God's consistent compassion for those who are victims of wrongdoing and injustice.

How is it possible for God to be perfectly merciful and perfectly just in dealing with undeserving, sinful human beings? Pope Paul VI described the human condition as a playing field between two extremes—between God's infinite love for humanity and our human misery (our pervasive wretchedness, distortion, and disconnection from the truth, goodness, and beauty of the one true God who created us in his image). God's ultimate expression of love is in Jesus Christ on the cross enduring the full brunt of human evil, insult, degradation, torture, and death for the sake of sinful, undeserving humanity. If that is not love, what is? God's self-emptying love is that by which he mercifully takes upon himself the judgment and punishment deserved by humanity. Justice is done by God, who shares human misery and takes the weight of human guilt upon himself to save humanity from destruction.

Where justice and mercy meet, there is peace! No real peace was achieved the day that Jacob was necklaced for his crimes. Jacob was a criminal, a poor, homeless, unemployed, and uneducated man. While none of this absolves him of responsibility or guilt for his crimes, the consequence he suffered at the hands of shopkeepers and the mob only compounded the wrongs of the day without setting things right all the way around. The questions in Jacob's case and in the case of every offender is how can justice be merciful; how can mercy be just?

The following chapter will consider these questions in relation to God's righteousness and what that means for us and all offenders.

CHAPTER 6

The Righteousness of God

Beyond Perfection

PRISONS SERVE A PURPOSE in society. One aspect of that purpose is to protect communities from crime and violence by segregating persons who are a threat or danger from the rest of the community. They are deprived of liberty. In that sense imprisonment serves as punishment for offenders, in part, to teach them a lesson and in part to deter others from offending. Although prisons are meant primarily as punishment and only secondarily for the rehabilitation of offenders, they are often referred to as correctional institutions (formerly also known as reformatories).

The idea is that by punishing offenders and providing them with opportunities for learning and counseling, their antisocial attitudes, values, and behavior can be corrected. For the most part however, rehabilitation is neglected due to cost and limited effectiveness.

A CURE FOR CRIME

Research on the impact of imprisonment on offenders reveals that an average of 70 percent of all offenders in prison have either been previously imprisoned or are likely to reoffend after being released. Because of imprisonment's dismal track record in correcting behavior, prisons are cynically dubbed "universities for crime." Prisons do not change the moral character of persons from "bad" to "good."

Frank is an offender who is considered incorrigible. He is an older man whose life of crime began with petty offenses when he was in his teens. Now, decades later, his life is marked by innumerable offenses and more than seventy convictions that have included several lengthy prison sentences. Frank has spent more of his life living inside a prison than outside. Within days of completing his most recent prison sentence he was no sooner out of prison than he committed another crime that resulted in him being arrested, charged with assault, and being locked up again. This is the story of his life and so far, no severity of prison sentence, psychological treatment, rehabilitation program, or remedial education has turned Frank into a law-abiding person. He is known as a habitual or hard-core repeat offender. While long-term repeat offenders like Frank represent a minority of prisoners, research indicates that the behavior of offenders cannot be changed simply through imprisonment and correctional plans. Something else needs to happen for their values, attitudes, and behavior to change.

During the final year of the Soviet Union, a high-ranking KGB official in Moscow who was responsible for the gulag prison camps was asked, "You've had virtually unlimited power and unquestioned authority in 'treating' prisoners. In your experience, have you found anything to be effective in changing lives for 'good'?"

After a moment of thoughtful silence, the officer looked up and said, "No, no—we have not found anything that is truly effective. I think it is because we forgot about 'the God.'" History shows that while government has the power to punish wrongdoing and restrain evildoers, government has neither the power nor the means to change the moral inclination of human beings from evil to good.

Two American researchers conducted a long-term study of serious criminal offenders to identify the key factors contributing to what they termed "the criminal personality."[1] Their premise was that if the cause of criminal behavior could be identified, the remedy or cure would follow. At the conclusion of their research, they found no significant evidence that criminality is correlated to external environmental, economic, educational, or other factors. The only common factor they discovered was the internal moral orientation, responsibility, and decision-making of the individual. This led them to suggest that the only possible solution to crime is the "moral conversion" of wrongdoers to a more responsible way of living.

THE HUMAN CONDITION

Frank has no desire to change his ways. As far as he is concerned, life is unrewarding and there is no point in being good. No one can tell Frank what to do—he is his own boss and he has his own ways. On the other hand, Eddie (the young man discussed in chapter 2) wants to change for good, but each time he is released from prison he finds it impossible to keep his resolve to change his ways. He ends up reoffending and being returned to prison.

St. Paul poignantly expresses the futility of human effort to become good:

> I do not understand what I do. For what I want to do I do not do, but what I hate I do. And if I do what I do not want to do, I agree that the law is good. As it is, it is no longer I myself who do it, but it is sin living in me. For I know that good itself does not dwell in me, that is, in my sinful nature. For I have the desire to do what is good, but I cannot carry it out. For I do not do the good I want to do, but the evil I do not want to do—this I keep on doing. Now if I do what I do not want to do, it is no longer I who do it, but it is sin living in me that does it. So, I find this law at work: Although I want to do good, evil is right there with me.[2]

1. Yochelson and Samenow, *Criminal Personality.*
2. Romans 7:15–21.

Human beings are created in the image of God and, unlike animals, they are endowed with conscious freedom, including freedom of choice and freedom of self determination. While animals are endowed with behavioral instincts in response to genetic imprinting and their environment, humans are endowed with the ability to make moral decisions.[3] While a great deal is known about psychological, social, and environmental factors that can influence moral behavior, we do not fully understand why people do wrong nor can we remedy an offender's propensity to do wrong apart from recognizing their human capacity to choose between good and evil. The biblical story of creation sets humankind in the garden, where they are free to obey or disobey God, their Creator.[4]

It is not uncommon to describe offenders who commit heinous acts of inhumanity like rape, murder, torture, and child abuse as being animals. However, they are not like animals acting by sheer instinct and outside a moral framework. They are human beings created in the image of God but who, for whatever reason, have turned toward evil. That is not to say that their behavior is only a matter of choice. There may be clear emotional, social, psychological, physical, or environmental factors involved. Something has gone terribly wrong, and society is at a loss to fully understand or repair that wrong. To relegate such an offender to animal status is to dismiss the painful reality that we are all human and the propensity toward evil is part of our human condition.

Not only violent and habitual offenders, but every human being grapples with those inclinations to do wrong. Since ancient times, wisdom Scriptures have noted that no one is perfectly good and immune to the possibility of evil:

"Behold, I was brought forth in iniquity, and in sin did my mother conceive me."[5]

---

3. The human ability to make moral decisions is, of course, affected by health, maturity, and complications of mental development, and other mitigating factors such as trauma. For a deeper discussion on approaches to moral reasoning see Groarke, *Moral Reasoning*.

4. Genesis 2–3.

5. Psalm 51:5.

"Indeed, there is no one on earth who is righteous, no one who does what is right and never sins."[6]

"The fool says in his heart, 'There is no God.' They are corrupt, and their ways are vile; there is no one who does good. God looks down from heaven on all mankind to see if there are any who understand, any who seek God. Everyone has turned away, all have become corrupt; there is no one who does good, not even one."[7]

ONLY GOD IS GOOD

As discussed in chapter 3, Scripture teaches that God is holy. By holy, among other characteristics, we recognize that God is morally perfect and untainted by the human condition. God has no tolerance for evil in himself and no accommodation for wrongdoing. The character of God is holy. The character of humans is sinful, and in exercising their freedom to make moral choices, humans have a bent to act against God. By disobeying God's moral commandments and by acting selfishly and hurtfully toward others, they turn their backs on God and on each other. From the beginning, all generations of humanity are tainted by sin, having inherited a propensity to make moral choices that are wrong and hurtful.

It is impossible for a person to undo this sinful disposition. Human nature cannot be put right or made holy by human beings who are themselves unholy and unrighteous. While *holy* refers to God's all-encompassing nature or essence, righteousness refers to the actions of God that flow from his nature.

Holiness and righteousness are inseparable aspects of God's nature. Holiness can only express righteous actions. Unrighteous actions cannot arise out of a holy nature. Compared to God, human attempts to attain righteousness fall short and are inadequate because of our unholy human condition. Isaiah poignantly expresses the futility of human efforts to save ourselves from the

6. Ecclesiastes 7:20.
7. Psalm 53:1–3.

human condition and become righteous: "How then can we be saved? All of us have become like one who is unclean, and all our righteous acts are like filthy rags; we all shrivel up like a leaf, and like the wind our sins sweep us away."[8]

GOD IS RIGHTEOUS

In previous chapters we discussed the fact that God's holiness is not a discrete trait in God's character, but is the essence of who God is. This makes him unlike (separate from) us humans. Therefore, unlike human love, justice, and mercy, God's love is holy love, God's justice is holy justice, and God's mercy is holy mercy. Because God is holy his love, mercy, and justice are perfectly linked together without any contradiction or competition between them. God's holiness is shown in the righteousness of all his actions. Extolling God's holiness in the consistency of his acts, the psalmist says, "The LORD is righteous in all his ways and faithful in all he does."[9]

Scripture also declares that God is both righteous and just in all he does: "Righteousness and justice are the foundation of his throne.[10] "The LORD Almighty will be exalted by his justice, and the holy God will be proved holy by his righteous acts."[11]

Depending on the English translation of the Greek and Hebrew words for righteousness, Scripture contains more than a hundred references to God's righteousness and the words *righteous* and *righteousness* are used nearly six hundred times. While the words *justice* and *righteousness* are not semantically connected in the English language, in Hebrew and Greek they are linked to the same word group. The Hebrew word *sedaqa* and the Greek word *dikaiousyne* can both be translated as righteousness or justice. In biblical usage, justice and righteousness overlap and at times are used synonymously. The same words used for justice and

8. Isaiah 64:5–6.
9. Psalm 145:17.
10. Psalm 97:2.
11. Isaiah 5:16.

righteousness denote not an ethical or moral standard but describe actions and behaviors that satisfy and issue from a relationship and are necessary for that relationship to flourish.

Righteousness primarily refers to God's action in saving his people. One of the clearest examples of this is the prophet Micah recounting and reminding the people how God's righteous acts rescued them from slavery:

> I brought you up out of Egypt and redeemed you from the land
>   of slavery.
> I sent Moses to lead you, also Aaron and Miriam.
> My people, remember what Balak king of Moab plotted
>   and what Balaam son of Beor answered.
> Remember your journey from Shittim to Gilgal,
>   that you may know the righteous acts of the LORD.[12]

In some translations, such as the Complete Jewish Bible, the phrase, "the righteous acts of the LORD" is expressed as "the saving deeds of the LORD." God's righteousness is expressed in rescuing a people who continually disobey and rebel against him. God acts to bring them back into relationship with himself by mercifully delivering them from judgment and graciously granting them a new status in that relationship. God's acts of compassion and mercy are righteous and call for an errant, disobedient, and rebellious people to repent and renew their commitment to live in relationship with him.

Upon reminding the people of God's righteous (saving) acts Micah also reminds them what God expects of them in that relationship. "And what does the LORD require of you? To act justly and to love mercy and to walk humbly with your God."[13]

CAN PERSONS BE GOOD WITHOUT GOD?

Fyodor Dostoyevsky, whose life was profoundly affected by exile and four years of hard labor in a Russian prison camp reflects on this question in his story of *The Brothers Karamazov*:

12. Micah 6:4–5.
13. Micah 6:8.

It's God that's worrying me. That's the only thing that's worrying me. What if He doesn't exist? . . . If He doesn't exist, man is the king of the earth, of the universe. Magnificent! Only how is he going to be good without God? That's the question. I always come back to that . . . after all, what is goodness? . . . one thing with me and another with a Chinaman, so it's relative. Or isn't it? Is it not relative? A treacherous question! . . . I only wonder now how people can live and think nothing about it. Vanity![14]

The self-help industry attests to the fact that people think they can become good through self-discipline, mindfulness, and efforts in self-improvement. Like many hard-driving individuals, Chuck Colson was determined to be a man of integrity and honor. He had a good upbringing, an excellent education. He was intelligent, disciplined, successful, and had a driving desire to live an exemplary life. But as conscientious and careful as he was, he could not sustain doing the right and the good he desired. Not all people end up being publicly disgraced and imprisoned for crime as he was, but everyone fails in living a completely good and morally upright life. Colson was ultimately convicted and sentenced to imprisonment for an illegal action he had justified in his own mind. Reflecting on his moral failure, he often said, "We are never more dangerous than when we are feeling self-righteous. We have an infinite capacity for this feeling and for the self-justification that accompanies it, and it is only when we turn to God that we begin to see ourselves as we really are—as fallen sinners desperately in need of His restraint and His grace."

Not only criminal offenders, but all human beings are incapable of becoming good by their own efforts. We are all imprisoned in the human condition from which it is impossible to extricate ourselves and from which we cannot possibly free others.

St. Paul bemoaned the futility of his effort to do the good he wanted to do and concluded that the only way out of his imprisonment in sin was through God's saving action: "I see another law at work in me, waging war against the law of my mind and making

14. Dostoevsky, *Brothers Karamazov*, 288–89.

me a prisoner of the law of sin at work within me. What a wretched man I am! Who will rescue me from this body that is subject to death? Thanks be to God, who delivers me through Jesus Christ our Lord!"[15]

RIGHTEOUSNESS AND JUSTIFICATION

Essentially, God's righteousness and God's justice are of the same substance. Describing God as righteous is not about some abstract moral characteristic or metaphysical quality of being. The righteousness of God describes God's unceasing actions in making right that which is wrong in the world. Justification is an English word that denotes this and is translated from the Greek word *dikaiosis*.[16] A better English word might be rectification, which captures the action of *dikaiosis* but gets lost in the word *justification*. Whereas justification implies a declaration of being made just, rectification implies the action involved in making things right or justifying, bringing together parts that have fallen out of line or that do not add up.

God is righteous in everything he does. Theologian Fleming Rutledge makes the case for God's acting in Jesus to set right what has gone so terribly wrong in humanity and which humanity is incapable of fixing.[17] God takes the initiative to rescue, redeem, reconcile, and restore sinful human beings into relationship. The righteousness of God is not a static state of being. Just as God has acted historically, he continues acting to restore humanity into relationship with himself. God opposes everything that resists his redemptive purpose for humanity.

When God acted in judgment against the rebellion and idolatry of Israel, he did not turn away from loving them, and his punishment of them was not for destruction but for their ultimate redemption and restoration. God takes initiative in righting the

15. Romans 7:23, 25.

16. As observed earlier, *dikaiosis is* derived from *dikaiosyne,* which can be translated as both justice and righteousness.

17. Rutledge, *Crucifixion.*

wrong that humanity cannot possibly correct or overcome. The prophet Hosea describes this righteous action of God as being like those of a loving parent:

> When Israel was a child, I loved him, and out of Egypt I called my son.
>
> But the more they were called, the more they went away from me.
>
> They sacrificed to the Baals and they burned incense to images. It was I who taught Ephraim to walk, taking them by the arms; but they did not realize it was I who healed them. I led them with cords of human kindness, with ties of love. To them I was like one who lifts a little child to the cheek, and I bent down to feed them. Will they not return to Egypt and will not Assyria rule over them because they refuse to repent? A sword will flash in their cities; it will devour their false prophets and put an end to their plans. My people are determined to turn from me. Even though they call me God Most High, I will by no means exalt them. How can I give you up, Ephraim? How can I hand you over, Israel? How can I treat you like Admah? How can I make you like Zeboyim? My heart is changed within me; all my compassion is aroused. I will not carry out my fierce anger, nor will I devastate Ephraim again. For I am God, and not a man—the Holy One among you. I will not come against their cities."[18]

God's righteous action also extends to those who are outside his covenant with the children of Israel, beyond their culture and their clans. The story of Jonah tells of God calling the people of Nineveh to turn from their wicked ways to be healed and brought into relationship with him. Although the Ninevites were enemies of Israel and known to be a sinful people who could not discern right from wrong,[19] God was concerned for their well-being and acted to save them. Like many people today, Jonah was adamant

18. Hosea 11:1–9.
19. Jonah 4:11.

that they should be punished and destroyed as evildoers and not be shown any mercy.

GOD IN HUMAN RUIN

God, who is holy and righteous, does not keep his distance from humanity inclined toward sin and evil, imprisoned in their human condition. Throughout history God repeatedly reaches out in judgment to draw people's attention back to him; and God intervenes in love to keep them from being completely overcome by evil. God's action in judgment and mercy is his cosmic work of justice and righteousness to set all things right. God comes down to live among human beings to show the depth of his unending love among those who are marginalized and oppressed.

In righteousness he assumes the burden of humanity's alienation and sin. In Jesus of Nazareth God becomes the unique human being to rescue, redeem, reconcile, and restore humanity. Jesus fulfilled and fulfills the prophecies of Isaiah that God will act righteously for all people and ultimately set all wrongs right.

> A shoot will come up from the stump of Jesse;
>> from his roots a Branch will bear fruit.
> The Spirit of the Lord will rest on him—
>> the Spirit of wisdom and of understanding,
>> the Spirit of counsel and of might,
>> the Spirit of the knowledge and fear of the Lord—
> and he will delight in the fear of the Lord.
> He will not judge by what he sees with his eyes,
> or decide by what he hears with his ears;
> but with righteousness he will judge the needy,
>> with justice he will give decisions for the poor of the earth.
> He will strike the earth with the rod of his mouth;
>> with the breath of his lips he will slay the wicked.
> Righteousness will be his belt
>> and faithfulness the sash around his waist.
> The wolf will live with the lamb,
>> the leopard will lie down with the goat,
> the calf and the lion and the yearling together;
>> and a little child will lead them.

The cow will feed with the bear,
     their young will lie down together,
     and the lion will eat straw like the ox.
The infant will play near the cobra's den,
     and the young child will put its hand into the viper's nest.
They will neither harm nor destroy
     on all my holy mountain,
for the earth will be filled with the knowledge of the LORD
     as the waters cover the sea.[20]

20. Isaiah 11:3–9.

CHAPTER 7

The Message of God
Beyond Words

A VOICE ECHOING IN sing-song cadence resounds through the prison courtyard. A visiting preacher is pacing back and forth. Surrounded by three tiers of overcrowded prison cells, the courtyard is empty in the afternoon heat. The prisoners are locked in their cells waiting for the daily head count to be completed. The captive audience is oblivious to the preacher's voice intermingled with the incessant clang and clamor of prison life.

PROCLAIMING THE WORD

The preacher comes to the congested Jamaican prison at the same time every week, always during the time inmates are locked down for the daily head count. He does not visit them in their cells and has no interest in meeting with individual prisoners, many of whom have been imprisoned for years without so much as a family visit. They are the forgotten ones: discarded, failures.

The preacher calls himself a prison evangelist.

"I come here to preach the gospel," he says emphatically. These men need to confess their sins and give their hearts to the Lord. I come to proclaim the message of repentance and salvation, the gospel of Jesus Christ for sinners!"

69

Every week he brings the same message, variations on the theme of judgment, heaven and hell, repentance, and salvation. There is no problem with his message as such. But the prisoners are unable to hear his words as good news. They already know that they are "as guilty as hell," they have already been judged and are being punished for their sins. They are marked as criminals and that will stain and blight the rest of their lives. No sermon in the world can change that reality for them.

What is the good news to men and women who are condemned by society? What is the good news of God for offenders who have a track record of failure and face the prospect of a dismal future? What news is so good as to compel people who feel angry, helpless, hopeless, humiliated, and alone to live in hope? The prison evangelist's message may be theologically correct: the only hope for a person in prison, as for any other person, is the good news of God's love, mercy, and grace. Yet the preacher's message does not penetrate the hard concrete and steel bars in which the hearts and lives of more than four hundred inmates are imprisoned.

Perhaps it takes more than words to convey God's love and mercy to disillusioned prisoners who are deprived of freedom and distanced from society.

MESSENGER AND MESSAGE

Marshall McLuhan, the communications specialist, observes that the medium or means of communication is often as powerful as the message itself. He suggests that the medium is the message, or at least an integral aspect of the message. Conflict or dissonance between the messenger and the message undermines the actual message and often renders it ineffectual. If the preacher in the courtyard had expressed God's love and care for the prisoners by taking an interest in their lives and personally engaging with them, his message would undoubtedly have found some traction. However, he offered them nothing beyond words echoing through an empty courtyard.

Meanwhile, on the other side of the world, a tall New Zealander with graying hair and a crinkly smile has just retired as an educator. Following a career that has taken him to Tonga as head of the education system, Peter and his wife return to New Zealand, where they plan to settle in their home by the sea. Unexpectedly, within months of retirement, Peter's wife passes away. As he begins picking up the pieces of his life, he considers the possibility of doing something completely different instead of just retiring. As he thinks back on his career, he recalls visiting a prison in Tonga to see how the prison teacher and students were faring. The reports had not been encouraging and he wanted to see for himself what was going on. He remembers the shock he felt at seeing the run-down prison conditions and inmates languishing amid deplorable, filthy cells. It was no wonder that the prison education program was a failure.

As the memories and images of that prison come back to Peter, he wonders if he should consider going back there to help the inmates and their teacher, as well as to share the message of God's love with them. Plans are made and he returns to Tonga where he meets with the prison director. The conditions of the prison are just as he remembered. Peter offers to help renovate the small prison classroom to create an environment more conducive to learning.

"Possibly I can even get the prisoners to help with the work," Peter suggests.

"You can certainly try, but it probably won't work," responds the director. "Why would they want to do anything—they are just waiting out their sentences."

Undaunted, Peter prepares a simple plan to clear out the accumulated debris in the classroom, repair the tables and chairs, replace broken windows, and paint the walls in a brighter color. Permission is granted for Peter to meet with the inmates about the project and about the value of education for life after prison. Some of the men are interested and he enlists them to organize small groups of inmates to take on the various tasks he has outlined. He leaves them with the tools and materials that will be needed.

A week later he returns to the prison only to find that the tools and materials have not been touched. Nothing has been done. The prisoners have no interest in fixing up the classroom or in learning. Peter is discouraged by their response. As he looks around at the conditions of the prison, and the cells in which the inmates live, he can understand how unmotivating it might be for the prisoners to repair a classroom when their own living conditions are in even greater need of repair. He decides, with the director's permission, to focus on improving the prison cells before the classroom. Once again Peter meets with the prisoners and tries to motivate and enlist them in the project, this time to clean, repair, and improve their living quarters to be more comfortable.

After another week he returns and finds the tools and materials are still untouched. Exasperated by the unresponsiveness of the prisoners, Peter feels that he needs to spend more time in the prison and requests permission to visit the prison daily and for longer times than the allotted two hours during the official visiting day each week.

"I am sorry, but that is not possible," responds the director. "Prison regulations only permit a once weekly two-hour visit."

"But there has to be a way," Peter counters. "Maybe I could come in as a volunteer chaplain or teacher."

"Only inmates and official prison staff are allowed inside. Even lawyers are restricted to the weekly visiting hours unless a judge orders otherwise."

"Well," Peter responds with temerity, "then I'll just have to become an inmate!" He is serious and after considerable negotiation Peter obtains special permission to move into the prison as a resident, subject to the same conditions, restrictions, and requirements as the inmates. It means he will be imprisoned for the duration of his stay.

Courageously, Peter accepts the conditions and moves into one of the empty prison cells. It is in terrible condition. He is alone and the reality of prison life becomes his reality. He is one of a hundred other inmates, eating the same food, living under the same conditions, and subject to all the rules and restrictions imposed by prison.

It is not an easy adjustment for Peter. After settling into his designated cell, he begins cleaning it up and making some basic repairs. Then he paints it. Some of the other prisoners begin commenting on the color and how happy it makes his cell look. They begin spending time with him and each afternoon he offers them tea. It is not long before several of them ask about making improvements to their own cells. Peter offers to help. As they spend more time together he gets to know them, and listens intently to their stories. He shares his own story and tells them about his experience of God's love and about Jesus.

As conversations grow, so does their work together. Gradually the prison is becoming a different place, conditions are improving, and the appearance is somehow brighter and more uplifting. The men too are changing as they become engaged in doing things for themselves and for each other. A small group of men are meeting regularly with Peter to learn about God his love for them. Through the radical act of sharing prison life with them, Peter is demonstrating God's boundless love for them. Now when Peter speaks, the prisoners listen and respond because they know he cares for them. They are hearing more than just his words.

LIVING THE MESSAGE

The message of God's redemptive love becomes discredited when those who bring that message do not respect or care about the people they are trying to reach. In most situations a message that is not lived falls on deaf ears. The message of God's love is negated when the messenger judges offenders as being unfit, useless, and unworthy. It is one thing to speak about love and quite another to care about a person who is unlikeable or difficult or even offensive. The message of God's love is magnified and made real when the messenger exhibits God's love in action.

Thomas Cranmer, the English reformer, called believers to a true and lively faith. By this he meant a faith that goes beyond mere belief to being put into practice as a way of life. James, one of the early apostles and possibly half-brother of Jesus, has this to say about the connection between faith and how we live:

> Do not merely listen to the word, and so deceive your-selves. Do what it says. Anyone who listens to the word but does not do what it says is like someone who looks at his face in a mirror and, after looking at himself, goes away and immediately forgets what he looks like. But whoever looks intently into the perfect law that gives freedom and continues in it—not forgetting what they have heard, but doing it—they will be blessed in what they do. Those who consider themselves religious and yet do not keep a tight rein on their tongues deceive themselves, and their religion is worthless. Religion that God our Father accepts as pure and faultless is this: to look after orphans and widows in their distress and to keep oneself from being polluted by the world.[1]

Unlike the prison preacher who passionately proclaimed "the word" but avoided relationships with prisoners, Peter left the comfort of home and retirement by moving into the confines of a miserable prison cell to share his life and faith with prisoners. It was one of the most difficult things he ever did, but it was a power-ful message bringing the words he spoke to life.

MESSAGE BEYOND WORDS

In both big and little ways, every messenger of God's love is called to embody, to live out the truth of the message. Sometimes the smallest acts of love and mercy convey a message far beyond any words that are spoken. This is particularly true among prisoners, men and women who feel judged, condemned, unloved, unwant-ed, hopeless, helpless, and worthless because that is how they are treated by society and the criminal justice system.

After passing through security in one of Latin America's most notorious prisons, a small group of prison volunteers, mostly older

1. James 1:22–27.

women, make their way through a series of long walkways lined with prison cells. The smells and sounds of Peru's Lurigancho prison are overpowering. As they pass by row after row of cells the women cheerfully invite prisoners to join them in the chapel for a Bible discussion and songs. Several volunteers carry guitars and other instruments; one of them strums lightly on her guitar as they walk toward the small chapel. A few inmates follow but many hang back in their cells. They have little interest in religion, even with music and the offer of cookies and soft drinks.

The chapel is a quiet place, a refuge from the noisy cells. As the visitors arrange chairs in a circle, they suddenly realize that Eva, one of the volunteers, is not with them. She came into the prison and through security with them but now she is nowhere to be seen. They are concerned and afraid because Eva is not well, having recently undergone chemotherapy and radiation treatment for cancer. This is her first time back in prison after a long time. Her friends had tried to stop her from coming but she insisted, "I must come, because I love the Lord and I love the prisoners."

Two of the volunteers retrace their way through the prison passageways and find Eva sprawled on the floor of a prison cell with a prisoner who is lying on the grimy concrete floor. They speak her name as they approach the bars of his cell. Eva motions for them to leave but they ignore her, fearing that she might be in danger. The cell belongs to Pablo, a notoriously disturbed young man who is known to be violent and suicidal. As the two volunteers cautiously step into the cell, they see that Eva is cradling his head on her lap. Tears are running down her cheeks as she softly whispers, "How dare you, how dare you try to end your life; it is such a precious gift from God. I am dying, my life is coming to an end. I would give anything to save it, but there is nothing I can do. You have your life. Do not destroy what God has given you. God loves you very, very much and so do I."

The two volunteers back slowly out of the cell and return to the chapel. For the next hour Eva remains on the grimy prison floor comforting Pablo and holding his head in her arms.

When Eva finally shows up in the chapel she tells the other women that she noticed Pablo curled in the fetal position on the floor when she walked by his cell. She overheard the prisoner in the adjacent cell sneer derisively that Pablo was "nothing but a piece of s---," a complete waste of time and breath. Eva stopped and asked him what was going on. The inmate said that nobody liked Pablo. There is something wrong with him and he tried to kill himself by drinking drain cleaner the previous day. After being attended to by the medics he had been dumped back into his cell.

Eva did not know and had never met Pablo. She had not even known his name before the inmate told her about him. It was then she felt God nudging her to go into his cell, and so she did. "Pablo could not come with us to the chapel, so I had to bring the chapel to him," she says.

Pablo was in no condition to comprehend Eva's message of life and love or grasp her words of comfort and affirmation. But one thing is for certain, Eva's humble presence beside him on the dirty concrete floor conveyed God's love for him beyond any of the words she spoke.

GOD'S WORD IS POWERFUL

The prison preacher at the opening of this chapter is convinced that all he needs to do is proclaim the word of God to the prisoners, nothing else.

"God's word is powerful," he says emphatically. "God says that his word will not return unto him void. 'The word of God is sharper than a sword, piercing the soul and the spirit.' It is not in my hands to do anything else; the word is powerful!"

The preacher is right, in a sense, even though the Scriptures he quotes are loosely taken out of context. However, for the message to be heard in the first place requires a messenger, and the role and demeanor of the messenger animates the message. Writing to the Romans, the apostle Paul depicts a certain beauty in the connection between the message and the messenger: "How, then, can they call on the one they have not believed in? And how can they believe in the one of whom they have not heard? And how can they hear without someone preaching to them? And how can anyone preach unless they are sent? As it is written: 'How beautiful are the feet of those who bring good news!'"[2]

The word of God, God's message, does not convey itself; it requires a messenger to articulate or animate the message. Paul shows the sequence by linking belief to hearing the message; and the message to a messenger; and the messenger to being sent. The role of the messenger is integral to the process. Paul echoes the words of Isaiah[3] in highlighting the significance of the messenger by describing their feet, the most mundane part of their body, as being beautiful. The messenger is integral to the proclamation and the hearing of the message. This does not mean that the response of the listener depends entirely on the messenger. Beyond the messenger and the message is the condition of the listener, the context in which the message is communicated, and the necessary work of the Holy Spirit, although the messenger still matters.

Of course, it is entirely possible that the message proclaimed by the prison preacher may find a response in the hearts and lives of some prisoners in spite of the disconnect between his actions and his message. At the same time Peter's message to Tongan prisoners was communicated more poignantly and powerfully because the words he spoke were underscored and authenticated when he moved into the prison to share his life with the inmates.

Pablo may have known that Eva was a "chapel person" but he would very likely never have been touched by the message in the chapel if she had not brought the chapel to him. By sitting down on the floor of his miserable cell, Eva conveyed God's word to him in a way that connected to his pain and isolation.

2. Romans 10:14–15.

3. Isaiah 52:7.

THE WORD OF GOD

People refer to the Bible as "the word of God" and so it is. Scripture refers to itself as God's word. Through historical narratives, recorded laws, poetry, wisdom literature, prophecy and apocalyptic visions, the Gospels, and the epistles, all biblical literature is considered God's message, the revelation of himself to humanity. As Paul wrote, "All Scripture is God-breathed and is useful for teaching, rebuking, correcting, and training in righteousness, so that the servant of God may be thoroughly equipped for every good work."[4]

The Bible also refers to "the word of the Lord" and "the Word of God" as a specific message given on a particular occasion. In the creation story God speaks and things come into being: "God said, 'Let there be light,' and there was light."[5] "God said, 'Let us make mankind in our image, in our likeness, so that they may rule over the fish in the sea and the birds in the sky, over the livestock and all the wild animals, and over all the creatures that move along the ground.'"[6] "By the word of the LORD the heavens were made, their starry host by the breath of his mouth."[7]

"The word of the Lord" also refers to God speaking to people in language they understand. In the very beginning God spoke to Adam, saying, "You are free to eat from any tree in the garden; but you must not eat from the tree of the knowledge of good and evil, for when you eat from it you will certainly die."[8] When God liberates Israel from slavery in Egypt, he speaks, reminding them that he is their God and the one who is delivering them: "I am the LORD your God, who brought you out of Egypt, out of the land of slavery."[9] When God gave the people instructions and

4. 2 Timothy 3:16–17.
5. Genesis 3:3.
6. Genesis 1:26.
7. Psalm 33:6.
8. Genesis 2:16,17.
9. Exodus 20:2.

commandments on how they should live, Exodus records that "God spoke all these words."

"The word of the Lord" also refers to messages God sends to his people through leaders, priests, and prophets, reminding them again and again of his decrees and of his covenant with them. Like other prophets, Jeremiah records "the word of the Lord" for the people: "The word of the LORD came to me, saying, 'Before I formed you in the womb I knew you, before you were born I set you apart; I appointed you as a prophet to the nations' . . . 'Alas, Sovereign LORD,' I said, 'I do not know how to speak; I am too young. But the LORD said to me, 'Do not say, I am too young. You must go to everyone I send you to and say whatever I command you.'"[10]

THE WORD AND THE MESSAGE

The biblical story is a story of the relationship between an infinite holy God and the people of his creation, a relationship marred from the beginning by unholy human wilfulness and disobedience, yet a relationship never abandoned by God. Within the context of the story is the central message of God's unending faithfulness and love for humanity. It is a relationship that God pursues through his mercy, justice, and righteousness. The Old Testament is the epic saga of a God who is ever true to his word and faithful to the promise of his covenant with human beings who turn out to be capricious, devious, and fickle—but people who are born free to reciprocate God's relationship with them, or not.

If the message of God's love can be distilled to its relational essence, it can be summed up in God's loving action and God's invitation to love: "For God so loved the world that he gave his one and only Son, that whoever believes in him shall not perish but have eternal life. For God did not send his Son into the world to condemn the world, but to save the world through him."[11] Jesus said, "Love the Lord your God with all your heart and with

10. Jeremiah 1:4–7.
11. John 3:16–17.

all your soul and with all your mind. This is the first and greatest commandment. And the second is like it: Love your neighbor as yourself. All the Law and the Prophets hang on these two commandments."[12]

From the beginning God has been true to his word. God's love for humanity did not change in reaction to their infidelities and insurrections. In an anthropomorphic sense, God remains totally devoted to bringing humanity back into relationship with himself despite their most dastardly and atrocious behavior. The Old Testament attests to the singular reality of God's unfailing love for humanity. God is faithful to his word, acting again and again to rescue and restore people to himself. God's love takes him to the ultimate expression of love when he assumes the finitude and frailty of being human. God enters into human history and our human condition to prove his love for all people in the depths of their experience; and on their behalf he takes upon himself the devastating burden and consequence of sin to prove his love, once-for-all overcoming sin's hold and power over life.

John captures the cosmic significance of God's Word coming into creation and being embodied in a human person to rescue humanity and restore humanity into relationship with himself:

> In the beginning was the Word, and the Word was with God, and the Word was God. He was with God in the beginning. Through him all things were made; without him nothing was made that has been made. In him was life, and that life was the light of all mankind . . . He was in the world, and though the world was made through him, the world did not recognize him. He came to that which was his own, but his own did not receive him. Yet to all who did receive him, to those who believed in his name, he gave the right to become children of God—children born not of natural descent, nor of human decision or a husband's will, but born of God. The Word became flesh and made his dwelling among us. We have seen his

12. Matthew 22:37–40.

glory, the glory of the one and only Son, who came from the Father, full of grace and truth."[13]

God became incarnate of the virgin Mary and was made man. In Jesus of Nazareth, a Galilean, God became a human being on the margins of society (see chapter 1). He was the embodiment of God's Word—the living message of God's love, proclaiming the good news of God's kingdom—the redemption, reconciliation, and restoration of all that has gone so horribly wrong among people and in the world. God gave himself as the Word, the message of his love in the life and death and resurrection of Jesus.

Long before God came down to earth, Isaiah foresaw the measure of God's love made visible through suffering on the margins of society:

> He was despised and rejected by mankind, a man of suffering, and familiar with pain. Like one from whom people hide their faces he was despised, and we held him in low esteem. Surely he took up our pain and bore our suffering, yet we considered him punished by God, stricken by him, and afflicted. But he was pierced for our transgressions, he was crushed for our iniquities; the punishment that brought us peace was on him, and by his wounds we are healed. We all, like sheep, have gone astray, each of us has turned to our own way; and the Lord has laid on him the iniquity of us all.[14]

God could have left humanity with only words recorded on a page or the words of an oral history. Instead, God went all in to show and tell the greatness of his love. He became the incarnate Word—messenger and message in the person of Jesus. When Peter moved into the Tongan prison, taking on himself the life of inmates, and when Eva sat on the floor of a filthy prison cell, the message they conveyed was motivated and empowered by God's love for the Tongan prisoners and for sick, suicidal Pablo.

13. John 1:1–14.
14. Isaiah 53:3–6.

CHAPTER 8

Jesus

The Living Word

"Can anything good come out of Nazareth?"[1] exclaims Nathanael, incredulous that his friend Philip presumes to have met God's promised Messiah, a man he identifies as Jesus from Nazareth. The very notion that the Messiah could come from a place like Nazareth seems preposterous. It is a place far removed from the center of religious and political influence and power, a "one-camel town" in Galilee, of all places. The promised deliverer could not possibly come from a backwater Jewish village surrounded by Gentiles in a region with ten Greek towns known as the Decapolis.

However, it soon becomes as evident to Nathanael as it is to Philip and his friends that Jesus is in fact the one sent from God. Everything Jesus says and does reflects the heart of God in ways that the prophets had foretold concerning the One who God would send to deliver his people. John's Gospel begins the story of Jesus' life with the poignant statement that "the Word became flesh and made his dwelling among us. We have seen his glory, the glory of the One and Only, who came from the Father full of grace and truth."[2] Another translation puts it this way: "And the word took human form and dwelt (tented) among us; and we saw his

1. John 1:45–47.
2. John 1:14.

preciousness (glory), a preciousness like that of an only beloved son of the Father, who is filled with loving kindness and justice."[3]

LOVE IN THE RUINS

Why would God, who is holy, deign to subject himself to mortal human flesh? Of course, there are various theological explanations of God's purpose in becoming incarnate in the person of Jesus. One of these explanations is the straightforward affirmation of John's Gospel that God became human in the person of Jesus because of his deep love for humanity, to save humanity. To do this God invested himself in the pathos, anguish, and fallenness of humanity, giving himself so fully so that all people might have life to the full. "For God so loved the world that he gave his one and only Son, that whoever believes in him shall not perish but have eternal life. For God did not send his Son into the world to condemn the world, but to save the world through him."[4]

Chorrillos prison for women (also known as Santa Monica prison) has been described as filthy, overcrowded, and disease-ridden, and as one of the worst prisons for women in Latin America. With limited toilet and shower facilities, as many as twenty or thirty prisoners use the same small washroom. Cells are often so overcrowded that inmates are forced to sleep on the floor. Built in the 1950s, Chorrillos was designed with capacity for three hundred inmates, however it frequently houses more than a thousand female prisoners, not including the young children who have nowhere to live other than in prison with their mothers.

It is not uncommon for women who have been charged with a crime to spend more than a year in Chorrillos before seeing a judge. They are considered guilty until proven innocent. Many are poor and unable to afford any legal help. Outside, their families tend to move on without them. A woman in prison or released from prison is considered "damaged." As a result, families break up

3. Lamsa, trans., *Holy Bible from the Ancient Eastern Text.*
4. John 3:16–17.

and move on, and when their prison time is done the women who are released have little hope and no way forward. Often the only alternative is sex work or the drug trade. For many women it is a depressing downward spiral.

The prison chapel in Chorrillos is a place of refuge and peace. Christian volunteers visit as friends to spend time with the women and offer them compassion, encouragement, and support. In the process many inmates become aware of God's love for them, as they learn about Jesus from these friends whose visits give them a sense of dignity and hope.

A large group of prisoners and prison visitors are gathering in the chapel. This is a special day because a group of inmates have written a play that they will be performing for the first time. The chapel is filling as the motley group of actors don their improvised costumes off to one side. The ten women who are performing the play have never acted before and are nervously excited. An expectant hush falls over the audience as the actors make their way to the front of the chapel.

Without any fanfare, the play comes to life as the actors noisily jostle, push, and shove their way onto the stage. It is quickly apparent that one woman is the focus of the commotion. Eight of the women dressed like men surround a provocatively dressed woman, pushing her, shouting, shaking their fists, and pointing their fingers at her in accusation. The woman is terrified, hair askew, makeup smudged, clutching a threadbare cloak to her body for dear life. She cowers before the "men" as they tower over her and push her to center stage. She stumbles under the crude force of their jostling. Fists shaking, fingers wagging, the accusations reach a frenzied crescendo—"Slut! Sinner! Whore! Trailer trash! Whore! Shame! Bitch!"

The poor woman is crying and shaking. The shouting stops, she drops to the ground quaking with fear as yet another "man" appears on stage. The accusers push her toward him with their feet, demanding that he tell them what should be done with this impure woman who has just been caught in an immoral act.

"The law requires death by stoning," they shout almost in unison.

"Stone her! Stone her! Stone her!," they chant. "She deserves to die!"

"What should we do, Jesus?"

The solitary actor looks down at the woman who is cringing at his feet. A crowd is gathering, and the man called Jesus stoops to the ground, kneeling in front of the woman so he can look into her face. He says nothing. Apart from a few coarse whispers, the accusers and the crowd fall silent as they watch him write something in the dust with his finger. Only the woman can see what he has written. Slowly he stands to his feet and looks around at the accusers.

"If any one of you is innocent and has done no wrong, you can be the first to throw a stone," he says, looking each one in the eye. The intensity builds as the "men" slowly back away. Then one by one they leave the scene. Only the woman and the man called Jesus remain on stage.

Suddenly the woman leaps to her feet and throws her arms around his neck. She is crying for real now, and so is "he." They are a mess of hugs and kisses. This is all unscripted and not the ending to the drama that anyone had planned. Nothing more needs to be said. Then all the actors return to the stage in tears, hugging each other and the woman they accused.

The drama tells their own story of rejection, humiliation, and anguish. Each of them, in one way or another, has experienced utter helplessness at the hands of a merciless justice system. Without someone to intervene on their behalf, someone who can see beyond the crime and treat them as a human being, they will be forever damaged and discarded.

Their prison drama is their depiction of Jesus publicly defending the life of a woman publicly accused of immorality.[5] It is a Gospel story that resonates with them, evidence of the love and mercy they are aching to experience in the ruins of their lives.

5. John 8:1–11.

THE SUBSTANCE OF A WORD

There is not much love lost for people who have committed crimes. Often even their own family members turn their backs on them. All the loving words once spoken do not hold up against wrongdoing, disappointment, and feelings of betrayal. All too commonly love is something much easier said than done.

The Hebrew term for "word" is *dabar*. It conveys "word" as having substance, implying the congruence of "word" with "deed." "Word" has substance in the same way as any other thing—as in "chair," which not an abstraction but has a corresponding substantive reality. Jesus, who is the Word, is not just an abstract message but the living substantiation of the word or message of God's love. Jesus is not some mystical representation of God's steadfast love, mercy, justice, and forgiveness; he is the corresponding reality of God's steadfast love, mercy, justice, and forgiveness. God's words are not disembodied ideas without substance, but express real things, most poignantly embodied in and through the person of Jesus. A true word is validated by its substance or action.

Eddie, the young inmate depicted in chapter 3, asks a piercing question: "Do you think God still loves me, even when I fail?" His question is the universal question of people who hear words of love but are not loved. It is all too easy to reassure someone like Eddie with words about God's love for him no matter what, then turn away from him with the empty sound of those words left behind. What Eddie needs is more than words about love, he needs to be loved for real.

In March 1997, three days after seven Israeli schoolgirls were brutally attacked and killed by a rogue Jordanian soldier, King Hussein of Jordan flew to Israel to visit the grieving families of those schoolgirls.[6] There was no talk of money or reparations. Instead, the king quietly sat down with the families, giving them his undivided attention. His unhurried and calm demeanor conveyed an empathy and solidarity with them that communicated far more

6. Reported in *The Los Angeles Times*, March 17, 1997, https://www.latimes.com/archives/la-xpm-1997-03-17-mn-39231-story.html.

than any words of sympathy. He was sympathetic. The families responded with profound appreciation and gratitude for the king's visit in their time of grief. They were deeply moved by the humble simplicity of his presence, an expression of his concern. That their grief and loss would be personally acknowledged and shared by the king who was considered an enemy of their people was unexpected. By humbly sitting with them, King Hussein touched them more deeply than any message of condolence. He was their comforter, sharing their pain and grief.

PUTTING FLESH TO WORDS

John Bunyan, author of *Pilgrim's Progress*,[7] was imprisoned in England's Bedford County Jail for more than twelve years. After his release from prison, he wrote this pointed reflection: "I know words are cheap, but a dram of grace is worth all the world."[8] Like most people in the depths of trouble and demeaning circumstances, he experienced the painful difference between cheap words of consolation and the consolation of those who do whereof they speak. It is the actions of those who love that communicate more deeply and profoundly than the most eloquent words that are only spoken.

John the Baptist was imprisoned after he criticized King Herod for consorting with the wife of his brother Philip. While languishing in prison John wonders if Jesus of Nazareth is truly the Messiah or not. Has John put his life on the line for just an idea, or is Jesus who he says he is? So, he sends two of his followers to put the question to Jesus directly: "Are you the one who was to come, or should we expect someone else?"[9] Jesus is not offended by the question and responds by pointing to his actions as proof of his message and his mission: "Go back and report to John what you have seen and heard: The blind receive sight, the lame walk, those

7. Bunyan, *Pilgrim's Progress.*
8. Bunyan, *Unsearchable Riches of Christ.*
9. Matthew 11:2–6.

who have leprosy are cured, the deaf hear, the dead are raised, and the good news is preached to the poor."[10]

Jesus' entire life is a proclamation of God's kingdom in word and deed. Everything he does embodies and enlivens the message of God's grace. From the prophecies of Isaiah to the song of Mary, Jesus puts flesh to (substantiates) the promise of God's justice, love, and mercy. There is no dissonance or discontinuity between Jesus' words and actions.

> His mercy extends to those who fear him,
>> from generation to generation.
> He has performed mighty deeds with his arm;
>> he has scattered those who are proud in their inmost thoughts.
> He has brought down rulers from their thrones
>> but has lifted up the humble.
> He has filled the hungry with good things
>> but has sent the rich away empty.
> He has helped his servant Israel,
>> remembering to be merciful
> to Abraham and his descendants forever,
>> just as he promised our ancestors.[11]

Jesus' words echo the prophecy of Isaiah when he speaks openly in the synagogue of his hometown: "The Spirit of the Lord is on me, because he has anointed me to proclaim good news to the poor. He has sent me to proclaim freedom for the prisoners and recovery of sight for the blind, to set the oppressed free, to proclaim the year of the Lord's favor . . . Today this scripture has been fulfilled in your hearing."[12] Despite the hostile response of the people, Jesus goes out from there to do exactly what he said.

The name "Jesus" means salvation and is derived from the Hebrew word *yeshua*. It is more than just a name, for everything Jesus says and does embodies God's attributes of steadfast love, mercy, justice, and righteousness. From his beginning in Nazareth,

10. Luke 7:18–22.

11. See Luke 1:46–55.

12. Luke 4:18–21.

he goes on to the towns and villages of Galilee, the Jordan, and to Jerusalem, consistently caring for the people he encounters, proving God's love for all people, even for Gentiles, Samaritans, and those who condemn him to death.

JESUS AT THREE MILES AN HOUR

Kosuke Koyama, a Japanese theologian, observes that even though Jesus is the "cosmic Christ," he becomes localized, the resident in a geography of small villages, living among people who know his name and his family. He is not anonymous; he is not an outsider. Jesus moves through his own village and goes from village to village at walking speed—three miles an hour, the average speed at which most people walk.[13]

As he walks through the countryside and the villages he is surrounded by people, including his disciples. Jesus proclaims the message of God's kingdom in their hearing, and in their presence he heals the sick, confronts evil spirits, and reaches out to sinners and Samaritans with dignity and respect. Jesus lives his entire life in plain view of people. He cannot escape or outpace his reputation. Everything he says is heard and everything he does is in plain view. News about him spreads and people follow him because he is trustworthy:

> Jesus went throughout Galilee, teaching in their synagogues, proclaiming the good news of the kingdom, and healing every disease and sickness among the people. News about him spread all over Syria, and people brought to him all who were ill with various diseases, those suffering severe pain, the demon-possessed, those having seizures, and the paralyzed; and he healed them. Large crowds from Galilee, the Decapolis, Jerusalem, Judea,and the region across the Jordan followed him.[14]

---

13. Koyama, *Three Mile an Hour God*.
14. Matthew 4:23–25.

There are of course, skeptics and naysayers, particularly among the Pharisees and teachers of the law, for whom the possibility that Jesus of Nazareth is God's Messiah is both preposterous and threatening. They repeatedly attempt to trip him up by looking for contradictions and inconsistencies between what he says and what he does. On the occasion that they confront Jesus with the woman caught in an immoral act, they lay a trap. "In the Law, Moses commanded us to stone such women. Now what do you say?" they demand.[15] It is a classic set-up; will Jesus do as God says? If he agrees to the stoning of the woman for her sins, that will go against everything he has been teaching about mercy and forgiveness. If Jesus objects to stoning her "as the law of Moses requires," then he will be undermining the moral law. Either way, they are sure this dilemma will cause Jesus to lose his credibility and spiritual authority. However, Jesus' response defuses their merciless judgment, by confronting the accusers with their own culpability and guilt.

WORKS OF GOD'S KINGDOM

Perhaps nothing incenses the religious purists more than when Jesus disregards the Sabbath laws in favor of healing and helping needy people. When Jesus restores mobility to the lame and the crippled, when he gives sight to the blind in the middle of the Sabbath, they call him out for breaking the law and acting contrary to God's will. This is the issue when Jesus heals a man who has been blind since birth.[16] At the time blindness was considered to be the direct consequence of sin, either the blind man's sin or that of his parents. The blind, the crippled, the leprous, and other diseased people were typically regarded as being spiritually and morally guilty—unclean.

When Jesus touches the blind man to heal him, he is not just defiling himself through contact with moral uncleanliness—it also

15. John 8:5.
16. John 9.

happens to be the Sabbath. Jesus is well aware of the fact that what he is doing will result in confrontation with the religious purists, the Pharisees. So, in reply to his disciples' question about sin in the man's life he says: "Neither this man nor his parents sinned . . . but this happened so that the work of God might be displayed in his life. As long as it is day, we must do the work of him who sent me."[17] Then Jesus spits on the ground, makes some mud, and applies it to the blind man's eyes. For the first time in his life the blind man can see. When the Pharisees investigate this and confront Jesus for breaking the Sabbath, he suggests that it is the Pharisees who are both guilty and blind to the ways of God.[18]

On yet another Sabbath when Jesus encounters a man who is suffering, he puts the question to the Pharisees, "Is it lawful to heal on the Sabbath or not?"[19] They do not answer. Then after healing the man, Jesus puts a question to them that confronts them with their skewed values and hypocrisy: "If one of you has a child or an ox that falls into a well on the Sabbath day, will you not immediately pull it out?"[20]

The Gospels of Matthew, Mark, Luke, and John each recount numerous stories of Jesus' mercy and compassion towards people in physical need. People who are suffering come to Jesus because they trust him to care and to help. On one of those occasions a group of men bring their paralyzed friend to Jesus.[21] His first words to the man are, "Friend, your sins are forgiven." The religious teachers and Pharisees immediately react, accusing Jesus of blasphemy because only God can forgive sins. Jesus responds to their criticism by asking, "Which is easier: to say, 'Your sins are forgiven,' or to say, 'Get up and walk'?"

Before any of them can answer the question, Jesus says, "But that you may know that the Son of Man has authority on earth to forgive sins . . ." and in the same breath he tells the crippled man to

17. John 9:3–4.
18. John 9:35–41.
19. Luke 14:1–6.
20. Luke 14:5.
21. Luke 5:17–26.

pick up his mat and go home. Everyone is amazed! Jesus' merciful act of healing has given weight to his words of forgiveness.

As poignant and powerful as Jesus' acts of physical healing are, his compassionate treatment of people who were morally, socially, ethnically, and religiously despised and marginalized is just as significant. Jesus embraces all people with respect and dignity—the poor, the morally unclean, Roman oppressors, obvious sinners, outcasts, and marginalized races. Jesus responds to those who are judged and vilified as reprehensible and unacceptable with compassion and love. Among them are:

- Despised tax collectors like Levi and Zaccheaus.[22]

- Marginalized Samaritans, including the woman at the well.[23]

- Outcast lepers, one also being a Samaritan.[24]

- Disreputable sinners like the woman caught in adultery, the woman who washed Jesus' feet with her tears, and sinners like tax collectors.[25]

- Terrifying people possessed by "unclean" and evil spirits, including the Gerasene demoniac living among the tombs, and Mary Magdalene.[26]

- Disregarded beggars like blind Bartimaeus and the helpless man at the pool of Bethesda.[27]

- Gentile overlords, including the Roman centurion whose daughter was ill and the Roman soldiers who crucified Jesus.[28]

No person, regardless of status or reputation, is beyond the embrace of Jesus; no one is excluded, no one avoided for being

22. Mark 2:13–17; Luke 9:1–10.
23. John 4:4–42.
24. Luke 17:11–17.
25. John 8:1–11; Luke 7:36–50; Matthew 9:10–17.
26. Mark 5:1–20; Luke 8:1–3.
27. Mark 10:46–52; John 5:1–17.
28. Luke 23:34.

unworthy, and no one is ever deemed to be above or beneath his concern.

A FINAL SCENE

The paperwork has just been completed and the incoming prisoner is informed of the rules for life in Humaita prison. Before taking the inmate to his assigned cell, the guard escorts him to the punishment cell. It is every prisoner's nightmare, and it is good for them to know what lies in store for them if they fail to follow prison rules or make trouble.

When they reach the cell, the guard opens the heavy steel door and gently pushes the prisoner into the dimly lit space. As the inmate's eyes adjust to the dim light, he expects to see the worst. Instead, there is a table with flowers and two small candles. On the bare concrete wall behind the table is a crucifix with the tortured figure of Jesus. Above the crucifix there is a simple inscription with just two words, "*Estamos Juntos*—We are Together." The prisoner does not know what to make of this. Behind him the guard says, "In this prison there will be no need for you to spend your time in punishment. Jesus is doing your time for you."

Entering the punishment cell of the APAC prison in Brazil introduces prisoners to a culture of compassion instead of judgment.[29] It introduces them to Jesus as the Savior who loves them

---

29. APAC is a Portuguese acronym that can be translated as "Loving Prisoners is Loving Christ." There are nearly fifty APAC prisons in Brazil, run by an association of Christian professionals and volunteers who are committed to treating criminal offenders as Jesus would. APAC operates as part of Prison Fellowship Brazil and serves all categories of convicted offenders, including those who have committed violent and serious crimes. Less than 5 percent of prisoners who are release from APAC re-offend (compared to 75 percent or more in the state prison systems). Prisoners are not referred to as inmates or prisoners but as *recuperandos*—persons in recovery. APAC prisons have no armed guards and for the most part it is trusted *recuperandos* who serve as staff and guards. For more information on this most unusual demonstration of Christian love for offenders, see https://www.americamagazine.org/politics-society/2021/11/17/brazil-alternative-prison-restoration-apac-241703 and https://justice-trends.press/the-apac-revolution-prisons-without-guards-without-police-without-weapons-

instead of the remote, moral judge they associate with religion and the church. In the APAC prison they are treated with respect, dignity, and love in the name of Jesus, who has completely given himself for them no matter what their crime or record. Jesus is the prisoner among them who takes all their guilt and punishment on himself, so they can be forgiven and have new life.

JUST BETWEEN THIEVES

APAC is the expression of good news for prisoners, that in Jesus, God is with them, not as judge but as fellow prisoner. Through APAC staff and volunteers Jesus relentlessly embraces the sorts of people who are not good enough to be included among the devout, proper, respectable, admirable, or rich and influential people. He is in prison with them sharing their burdens and pain, *Estamos Juntos.*

In an essay, G. K. Chesterton refers to Jesus as representing "the furious love of God."[30] Jesus states in no uncertain terms that he has come "to seek and to save the lost."[31] When Jesus is criticized by the "upright" and uptight people of society and their religious leaders for spending time eating and socializing with the likes of disreputable tax collectors and sinners, he tells them, "It is not the healthy who need a doctor, but the sick. I have not come to call the righteous, but sinners."[32]

Despite all the criticism, opposition, and threats against him, Jesus never wavers in his compassion and mercy for troubled people and those in trouble. It is not enough that Jesus verbally proclaims God's love to undeserving offenders, he loves them. This gets Jesus into trouble. Then as now, folks tend to look down on people whose foibles, faults, and failures are public and blatant— criminals and prisoners. Ultimately God's love is not abstract

---

without-violence-without-corruption-without-drugs-without-discrimination/.

30. Chesterton, "Diabolist."

31. Luke 18:10.

32. Mark 2:16–18.

words written on a page or spoken, it is God's love enacted in Jesus who responds to the deepest human need, failure, and disgrace.

BELIEVE IT OR NOT

After being with Jesus for three years, following him through the towns and villages of Galilee, down to the Jordan, and into Samaritan territory, his disciples have heard Jesus' words again and again. They had seen his love and compassion expressed in amazing acts of mercy and grace. Things are coming to a head as they accompany Jesus to Jerusalem, where, he tells them, he will be facing death. They do not know quite what to make of this. It is not the way they see things playing out, and there is one thing they need to know, one big question on their minds. Jesus tells them that he is going to the Father, but they wonder where God is in everything that Jesus has been teaching and doing. Philip expresses what is on their minds

"Show us the Father," Philip says to Jesus, "and that will be enough for us."

"Don't you know me," replies Jesus, "even after I have been with you for such a long time? Anyone who has seen me has seen the Father."[33]

And there they have the answer. Everything Jesus says and does is what the Father does.

Jesus continues, "The words I say to you are not just my own. Rather, it is the Father living in me, who is doing his work. Believe me when I say that I am in the Father and the Father is in me; or at least believe on the evidence of the miracles themselves."

Now they catch a glimmer of what God is doing—the miracles are not just miracles, they are evidence, validating the good news of God's unending love for all people, bent and broken as they are.

"If you love me," Jesus tells them, "you will obey what I command . . . If anyone loves me he will obey my teaching. My Father will love him, and we will come to him and make our home with

33. John 14:5–14.

him . . . These words you hear are not my own; they belong to the Father who sent me."[34]

And so it is, when they reach Jerusalem the upright insiders who want a Messiah in their own image reject Jesus. He is betrayed, falsely accused, arrested, interrogated, tortured, sentenced, and executed just like a common criminal offender, because his way of life confronts the hypocrisy of their religious ways of believing in God to the neglect of pursuing God's will and way of mercy, love, and justice.

It is no accident that Jesus' life ends in the company of thieves, with a criminal crucified on either side of him. And even in the agony of mistreatment and death Jesus forgives the soldiers who are dividing his clothes. As onlookers sneer at him and mock him, one of the criminals recognizes Jesus as being unjustly executed, while he and the other criminal are guilty. "Jesus, remember me when you come into your kingdom," is his dying plea.

Jesus answers, "Truly I tell you, today you will be with me in paradise."[35]

Legend refers to this criminal as "the Good Thief" and ascribes him the name Dismas. Whether that was his name or not is of little consequence. What is significant is that Jesus offers mercy to a criminal in his dying hours. Jesus' final act is to forgive both his executioners and a convicted criminal.

EPILOGUE

No one understands the significance of this more deeply than Paul, who was the relentless persecutor of those who believed and followed Jesus as Lord. When he comes face-to-face with God's love in the crucified and risen Jesus, Paul's life is shaken to the core and he is never the same. Instead of persecuting those who followed the Way of Jesus, he becomes one of them. For this he is persecuted and imprisoned. From prison, Paul writes a letter to

34. John 14:14; 23–24.
35. Luke 23:42–43.

his fellow believers, affirming the awesome nature of God's love made real in and through Jesus' selfless love for offenders—sinners just like him.

> You see, at just the right time, when we were still power-less, Christ died for the ungodly. Very rarely will anyone die for a righteous person, though for a good person someone might possibly dare to die. But God demon-strates his own love for us in this: While we were still sinners, Christ died for us.[36]

36. Romans 5:6–8.

CHAPTER 9

Jesus
The Truth of God

ROGER IS IN PRISON, considered a dangerous terrorist. He is only allowed out of his small solitary cell once a week. He cannot associate with other prisoners and so he uses the time going to the tiny prison library. He is a passionate, young student revolutionary and radio commentator who is committed to the cause of justice for his poor Filipino people suffering under the oppression of the corrupt Marcos regime.[1] Marcos has declared martial law, using the armed forces to impose his power over the country. Since Roger is notorious for his bombastic rhetoric and use of explosive tactics against the regime, the news media dubs him Roger "Bomba" Arienda. He is among the most wanted men in the Philippines.

Then, during a military operation, he is captured and finds himself locked up. This is not Roger's first stint in prison. He has been imprisoned before but escaped. But this time he faces a harsher sentence under tight security in a solitary cell. He is too inflammatory to be allowed contact with other prisoners.

Armed officers escort "Bomba" on his weekly visit to the prison library. Once inside he looks around for books that he has not read. He is hoping to find something in keeping with his political passion and thirst for justice. There isn't much until he sees

1. https://www.britannica.com/biography/Ferdinand-E-Marcos.

a book with a red cover hidden beneath a pile of tattered novels. Immediately he recognizes it as being "The Little Red Book" of the revolutionary sayings of Chairman Mao Zedong, the leader of the communist revolution in China.[2]

Thrilled with his find, Roger tucks the book in his shirt and is escorted back to his cell. Eagerly he pulls out the book, only to discover that the book with the red cover is not what he thought it was. He has made a dreadful mistake. The bright red book is a copy of the Gospels. Disappointed and furious, Roger throws the book into the corner of his cell. Religion is not the answer to the political corruption of the Philippines! If anything, religion is part of the problem. It is the establishment.

A TRUE REVOLUTIONARY

A day passes and now Roger is totally bored. With nothing to do and nothing else to read until he can go back to the library next week, he picks up the red book and begins reading. Before the week is out Roger has read the book several times. He is becoming increasingly captivated by the story of Jesus, discovering that he is not the person of religion he expected him to be. In the story of Jesus' life and teachings, Roger sees someone far more radical than he thought, far more radical than the church made him out to be.

Roger encounters Jesus as someone who identifies with poor and oppressed people, people who are marginalized and put down by the powers that be and by the religious establishment. Jesus' teachings and way of life are revolutionary, but instead of rhetoric inciting one group or class of people against another, Jesus invites people to a way of justice and mercy, love, and forgiveness. Jesus actually lives out his ideal.

This understanding of Jesus completely blows Roger's mind. When he comes to the story of Jesus forgiving the people who have conspired against, maligned, and tortured him, Roger knows he has met someone who is different from Chairman Mao or any of

2. Tse-Tung, *Quotations from Chairman Mao.*

his other revolutionary teachers and heroes. He encounters Jesus as a different kind of revolutionary and realizes that the revolution he has been so passionate about will ultimately not change anything. It will only turn the tables of power and oppression without changing the underlying causes of injustice, discrimination, and corruption. The oppressors of today will become the oppressed tomorrow; and the oppressed today will become their oppressors. It is a desperate vicious cycle of violence that will never lead to justice and freedom for all.

Roger sees that Jesus' way of love and forgiveness is not idealistic revolutionary rhetoric. Jesus' way of life has integrity. On the one hand, he is not intimidated, nor does he cut deals with the Roman oppressors of his people. Nor does he react to the enemies of his people with disrespect or violence. On the other hand, Jesus does not avoid taking issue with the religious leaders of his people who withhold justice and treat others without being merciful and loving. He confronts them for exploiting their positions for personal gain at the expense of the poor and marginalized. Jesus pulls no punches and practices what he preaches, no matter who is listening or watching. The revolutionary teachings and way of Jesus are liberating for all.[3]

From his own imprisonment, Roger resonates with John the Baptist's burning question of Jesus: "Are you the one who is to come, or should we expect someone else?"[4] John knows Jesus has proclaimed "freedom to the prisoners and liberation for the oppressed,"[5] but now he is languishing in prison under Herod's thumb. Is Jesus really the Messiah? It is a question of integrity. Can Jesus be trusted or are his words empty? Jesus responds to John's question by pointing to the evidence and sends the messengers back to John to report what they have seen and heard.

Roger can see that Jesus is not saying one thing and doing another, nor is he just saying something and doing nothing. Repeatedly the religious leaders and the Pharisees ask Jesus for a sign

3. Arienda and Roque-Lutz, *Free Within Prison Walls.*

4. Luke 7:19.

5. Luke 4:8.

to prove that his teaching is trustworthy and authoritative. Jesus refuses to prove himself on demand, because everything he does is evidence enough. This is compelling, and Roger comes to believe that Jesus is trustworthy.

A MATTER OF INTEGRITY

Jesus' life and message would have been dismissed and discredited if he had been inconsistent or hypocritical. Jesus lived his life in public view. Despite every effort to put him down, and prove him wrong, his detractors can find no fault of word or action in his life, no "dirt" of untruth or deception.

Like the people in his family and church, Stu also believes in Jesus. Stu is brilliant, likeable, fun-loving, witty, generous person who is a loving father and works to provide the very best for his family. He is the kind of man people are proud to have as a friend—until the day they discover that he is a fraud, a man without integrity.

Since childhood, Stu's dream was to become a medical doctor, to help suffering people. After years of study he finally achieves his dream. After completing medical school he is appointed to a leading position with a prestigious hospital. Stu is doing what he has always dreamed of, helping people get well. His reputation as a doctor is growing, but there is a problem.

As generous and caring as Stu seems to his patients, he is becoming more concerned about his reputation and his own well-being than that of his patients. He is helping them get well, but that alone is not enough. He wants to be rich. Stu seems compassionate and giving on the outside, but inside he has an insatiable hunger for the good things in life: the best food, the finest wines, expensive cars, first-class travel to world-class cities, and the most luxurious house in one of the most exclusive neighborhoods. Gradually he begins turning away from treating patients to putting more time and effort into opportunities to make money.

Stu does not completely turn his back on caring for others. He does charitable medical work by going on medical mission trips to places of conflict and need. It serves him well to be recognized for his generous and compassionate service. It is an image he cultivates even as he devotes his energy to pursuing investment opportunities and cutting deals. Stu moves among some of the wealthiest investment bankers and fund managers in the country. He is smart, persuasive, and most of all he has a knack for recognizing investment opportunities in the field of pharmaceutical and medical innovations.

As the opportunities grow more complex and riskier, Stu begins crossing the lines of integrity and ethical responsibility. Convinced that he is smarter than anyone else, he deftly manipulates inside information and induces experts to protect the value of the investments he is overseeing.

Stu believes in the virtue of honesty and teaches his children to tell the truth. But what he believes is not reflected in his ways of doing business. Stu also values compassion and caring, but his dishonesty and greed are beginning to hurt the investors and business partners who trust him. Eventually they will lose a lot of money because of him.

Everything unravels as his inconsistencies and financial manipulation come to light. When Stu is arrested and charged with fraud and obstruction of justice, angry co-workers call him a faithless servant who has no integrity. Neighbors and former friends shun him as a disgrace to the community. He is unable to cover up the truth of who he really is and what he has been doing. Stu is found guilty and sentenced to prison. The truth he believed about Jesus, and affirmed, had not infected his way of life and he was found out.

THE WHOLE TRUTH

Truth and integrity are inseparable. When a person gives testimony in a court of law, that person is sworn to tell the truth, the whole truth, and nothing but the truth. The testimony of that person is expected to be complete and unbiased without anything false being added or anything true deleted. Most people may not be publicly humiliated for their lack of integrity like Stu, but they are inconsistent and the truth about them is seldom on public display. People tend to lie and cover up their actions to protect themselves, and create false impressions in order to gain attention and respect. It often doesn't hold.

The Gospels describe Jesus as being a person who is completely true and on full display—Jesus is filled with truth, he speaks the truth, he leads to truth, he is portrayed as being the truth, he openly declares that his purpose is to witness to the truth of God. From beginning to end the veracity and trustworthiness of his life and witness holds up to scrutiny.

- The beginning of John's Gospel identifies Jesus as being filled with truth: "the one and only Son, who came from the Father, full of grace and truth."[6]

- Jesus identifies as one being truthful and trustworthy, the very opposite of Satan, who is the father of lies. "He was a murderer from the beginning, not holding to the truth, for there is no truth in him. When he lies, he speaks his native language, for he is a liar and the father of lies. Yet because I tell the truth, you do not believe me! Can any of you prove me guilty of sin? If I am telling the truth, why don't you believe me? Whoever belongs to God hears what God says. The reason you do not hear is that you do not belong to God."[7]

- Jesus says that those who believe him and follow his teaching will know the truth: "To the Jews who had believed him, Jesus said, 'If you hold to my teaching, you are really my disciples. Then you will know the truth, and the truth will set you free.'"[8]

- Jesus publicly declares that his mission is to testify to the truth: "The reason I was born and came into the world is to testify to the truth."[9]

6. John 1:14.
7. John 8:44–47.
8. John 8:31–32.
9. John 18:37.

- Jesus' detractors admit that what Jesus teaches is true: "So the spies questioned him: 'Teacher, we know that you speak and teach what is right, and that you do not show partiality but teach the way of God in accordance with the truth.'"[10]

- Jesus categorically declares that he is "the truth," thereby identifying himself with the Father: "I am the way and the truth and the life. No one comes to the Father except through me. If you really know me, you will know my Father as well."[11]

THE WAY OF TRUTH

When Jesus is falsely accused, arrested, and arraigned before Pontius Pilate, the Roman governor, truth is at stake. Under questioning, Jesus responds to Pilate by saying that he has come to testify to the truth. In response to Jesus Pilate asks, "What is truth?"[12]—as if there is a possibility that truth can have different definitions or shades of meaning.

Unlike Greek philosophical notions of truth, the Hebrew understanding of truth does not define something as true simply by its correspondence to reality or logic. Truth is much more than that. The Hebrew word for truth is *emmet*, the connotation of which is all-inclusive. Some rabbinical scholars point out that *emmet* begins with the first letter of the Hebrew alphabet, ends with the last letter, and therefore truth is everything contained between the beginning and the end.[13]

10. Luke 20:21.

11. John 14:6–7.

12. John 28:28–40.

13. Some rabbinical scholars note the first letter of *emmet* is not only the first letter of the alphabet, but the letter also stands for "One" as in "the Lord our God is ONE." Thus, it stands for God. However, if the first letter is removed from *emmet*, the resultant word means "death." Truth originates in God and that apart from the one and only God there is no truth, only death—nothing.

Jesus is the revelation of God who is the beginning and the end, the Alpha and Omega, containing everything that is from the beginning and that which is yet to come[14] Jesus is the truth.

Jesus unequivocally declares, "I am the way and the truth and the life. No one comes to the Father except through me. If you really know me, you will know my Father as well. From now on, you do know him and have seen him."[15] In healing the sick, forgiving the sinful, delivering the demon-oppressed, feeding the multitudes, befriending the marginalized, respecting the outcast, and dignifying the poor, Jesus evidences the truth and the true way of God's love and mercy toward all. In all his teachings, parables, and conversations with people, Jesus expresses the true loving, merciful, just, and righteous way of the Father. The interweaving of Jesus' actions and teaching is the consistent, true message reflecting the heart and character of God.

The Truth of God's Love

Love is the core of what Jesus teaches and reveals about God. When Jesus is questioned about the relative importance or priority of God's commandments he states that it begins and ends with love: "'Love the Lord your God with all your heart and with all your soul and with all your mind.' This is the first and greatest commandment. And the second is like it: 'Love your neighbor as yourself.' All the Law and the Prophets hang on these two commandments."[16] When someone asks Jesus to clarify who is included or not included as a neighbor, he replies by telling the story of a Samaritan traveler who responds with compassion and generosity in caring for a wounded stranger who is bypassed and abandoned on the roadside by others.[17] Jesus is pointing not to who might or might not be included as a neighbor but to the response of someone who

14. See Revelation 1:8, 17; 21:6; 22:13.

15. John 14:6–7.

16. Matthew 22:37–40.

17. Luke 10:25–37.

sees a person in need or trouble. Loving as God loves has nothing to do with who is a literal neighbor and everything to do with the response of the person to someone in trouble.

Jesus teaches that God's way of love is tenacious, as in a woman's search for an insignificant lost coin; compassionate as in a shepherds' search for just one lamb of many that has gone astray; and forgiving as in the response of a waiting father who joyfully, unreservedly embraces and celebrates the return of his willful, disrespectful son.[18]

There are no limits to God's way of love expressed in friendship that prefers the other at personal cost and sacrifice.[19] Such love is not confined to mutual friendships and reciprocal relationships but is most profoundly expressed in forgiving, caring, and praying for those who are outside the circle of friendship, even those who are offenders and enemies.[20]

Those who walk and live in the way of God's love do so in fellowship and communion with him.[21] For it is in loving others unreservedly and unconditionally that we show the world that we are living in the embrace of God.

The Truth of God's Mercy

Jesus teaches that God is merciful, and that mercy is what he desires from those who have received his mercy. There is a connection between God's mercy toward us and our expressions of mercy toward others: "Blessed are the merciful, for they will be shown mercy;"[22] "Be merciful, just as your Father is merciful."[23]

Jesus shows that God's way of mercy goes beyond expressions of sympathy or feelings of pity. Like love, mercy is expressed

18. Luke 15.
19. John 15:9–17.
20. Matthew 5:43–48; Luke 6:35–38.
21. John 14:15–21.
22. Matthew 5:7.
23. Luke 6:36.

and proven in acts of caring for and helping someone in need and trouble, without regard to their status or whether or not they are deserving. In responding to the Pharisees who were zealous in keeping the law and quick to pass judgment on those who break the law, Jesus teaches that being merciful toward others, including offenders, is infinitely more important than passing judgment on them.[24]

Near the end of his life Jesus tells a parable of what the kingdom of God is like. The story he tells is one in which mercy is the measure of those who are aligned with him and welcomed into the kingdom. Jesus portrays them as people who are moved with love, compassion, and mercy to feed the hungry, give water to the thirsty, clothe the naked, care for the sick, and visit prisoners. God's way of mercy is demonstrated through the actions of merciful people who are caring and compassionate toward others without expecting recognition or reward.[25]

Forgiveness also expresses God's mercy and grace. God's way of mercy offers forgiveness to all offenders.[26] When Peter asks Jesus about the limits on forgiving someone, Jesus replies that forgiveness goes beyond any of the limits he might be inclined to use. Jesus shows a limitless mercy when he expresses forgiveness to the soldiers who have mocked and tortured him, who are crucifying him and casually gambling for his clothing as he suffers in naked agony on the cross.[27]

The Truth of God's Justice

John's Gospel opens with the proclamation that Jesus' mission in response to sin and evil is to bring salvation to the world, not to condemn the world: "God did not send his Son into the world to

---

24. Matthew 23:23.
25. Matthew 25:31–46.
26. Matthew 6:14.
27. Luke 23:34.

condemn the world, but to save the world through him."[28] Jesus enacts the justice of God by attending to the sick and sinners as an expression of God's love and mercy. God's way of justice comes by way of grace extended to those who deserve punishment, in order to save, redeem, reconcile, and restore them into relationship with God. When the Pharisees criticize Jesus for socializing with tax collectors and sinners, Jesus replies, "It is not the healthy who need a doctor, but the sick. I have not come to call the righteous, but sinners."[29]

God's way of justice is not like our way of justice. He does not condemn and reject guilty offenders but reaches out to them with forgiveness. Jesus points out this difference in teaching us not to be judgmental of others: "Do not judge, and you will not be judged. Do not condemn, and you will not be condemned. Forgive, and you will be forgiven."[30] Where our natural response to injustice, injury, and loss at the hand of another is to seek retribution, revenge, and punishment, Jesus says that justice is not accomplished through retaliation, even if retaliation is restrained as in an eye for an eye or a tooth for a tooth. Justice is not a balance where violence is resolved through violence. Rather, Gods' way of justice is a gracious response rooted in love for the other.

> You have heard that it was said, "Eye for eye, and tooth for tooth." But I tell you, do not resist an evil person. If anyone slaps you on the right cheek, turn to them the other cheek also. And if anyone wants to sue you and take your shirt, hand over your coat as well. If anyone forces you to go one mile, go with them two miles. Give to the one who asks you, and do not turn away from the one who wants to borrow from you. You have heard that it was said, "Love your neighbor and hate your enemy." But I tell you, love your enemies and pray for those who persecute you, that you may be children of your Father in heaven.[31]

28. John 3:17.

29. Mark 2:17.

30. Luke 6:37.

31. Matthew 5:38–44.

The Truth of God's Righteousness

Jesus teaches that God's way of righteousness is more than a matter of right belief or moral purity. It is about pursuing a right relationship with God and with others. The Pharisees and religious leaders were notorious for pursuing the letter of God's law. Yet they were missing the higher purpose of God's will, his intention for humanity. Jesus elevates the understanding of righteousness to a higher standard: "I tell you, unless your righteousness exceeds that of the scribes and Pharisees, you will never enter the kingdom of heaven."[32]

On one occasion Jesus addresses the false notion of righteousness practiced by the scribes and Pharisees, by calling them out for their onerous religious practices at the expense of pursuing justice and mercy in their relationships with others:

> Do not do what they do, for they do not practice what they preach. They tie up heavy, cumbersome loads and put them on other people's shoulders, but they themselves are not willing to lift a finger to move them. Everything they do is done for people to see . . . Woe to you, teachers of the law and Pharisees, you hypocrites! You give a tenth of your spices—mint, dill, and cumin. But you have neglected the more important matters of the law—justice, mercy, and faithfulness. You should have practiced the latter, without neglecting the former.[33]

In his Sermon on the Mount,[34] Jesus pronounces blessing on people who hunger and thirst for righteousness, and on those who are persecuted on account of their righteousness. The actions of righteousness, including mercy and peace, are bracketed between these two statements.[35] God's way of righteousness is the relational way of mercy and justice.[36] Both mercy and peacemaking, as well as

32. Matthew 5:20.
33. Matthew 23:3–5; 23.
34. Matthew 5.
35. Matthew 5:7–9.
36. See chapter 7 on peacemaking as the action of justice, by which wrongs

justice, center on purity of heart,[37] which is considered the core of the Beatitudes. Purity of heart is moral and spiritual integrity before God that proves itself in right behavior toward and right relationships with others. In purity of heart and lifestyle there is no discontinuity or hypocrisy between a person's faith and relationship with God, and their relationships with and attitudes toward others.

> Blessed are those who hunger and thirst for *righteousness*,
> for they will be filled.
> Blessed are the *merciful*,
> for they will be shown mercy.
> Blessed are the *pure in heart*,
> for they will see God.
> Blessed are the *peacemakers*,
> for they will be called children of God.
> Blessed are those who are persecuted because of *righteousness*,
> for theirs is the kingdom of heaven.

Jesus is the true Word of God. He is the way, the truth, and the life. Jesus perfectly represents the heart of God the Father and the presence of his kingdom.

> For I did not speak on my own, but the Father who sent me commanded me to say all that I have spoken. I know that his command leads to eternal life. So whatever I say is just what the Father has told me to say.[38]
> The words I say to you I do not speak on my own authority. Rather, it is the Father, living in me, who is doing his work. Believe me when I say that I am in the Father and the Father is in me; or at least believe on the evidence of the works themselves . . . Anyone who loves me will obey my teaching. My Father will love them, and we will come to them and make our home with them. Anyone who does not love me will not obey my teaching. These words you hear are not my own; they belong to the Father who sent me.[39]

---

are made right in reconciling relationships and the restoration of well-being (*shalom*).

37. Matthew 5:8.
38. John 12:49–50.
39. John 14:10–11; 23–24.

CHAPTER 10

Jesus
The Way of God's Kingdom

IN A COUNTRY WRACKED by crime and violence, where criminals are feared; where prisoners are hated and mistreated, where prisons do nothing to break the cycle of crime, and where the courts are a revolving door of repeat offenders—four Brazilians believed there was a better way of responding to crime and criminals. They took Jesus at his word when he said, "I was in prison you came to visit me . . . Come, you who are blessed by my Father; take your inheritance, the kingdom prepared for you since the beginning . . ."[1]

ACTS OF THE KINGDOM

The four Brazilians agree to put their faith into action. They are familiar enough with the growing crime crisis and the challenges of working with criminal offenders. Among the members of the group are a judge, a lawyer, a psychologist, and a reporter. They are not naïve in going to prison to visit a group of prisoners who have been convicted of serious crimes. The inmates don't get very many visitors at all. Most people, including many family members, refuse to have anything to do with them.

1. Matthew 25:36, 34.

After several months of regular visits, during which they have come to know the prisoners they form an association calling themselves APAC. It is a Portuguese acronym standing for "*Amando al Preso, Amando el Cristo*, Loving the Prisoner is Loving Christ."

Years have now passed since the group began their visits. Prisoners' lives are being transformed, the cycle of crime is being broken, and the prisons they visit are changing for the better. Hundreds of people across Brazil have joined them in a movement touching prisoners and prisons with the love of Jesus expressed through practical care and friendship. The real power of the movement is not in its organization, or the number of people involved. The real power is in followers of Jesus expressing God's love in action, treating imprisoned offenders, both men and women regardless of the nature of their crimes, with respect, dignity, and compassion. The movement has had such a remarkable impact that the government is turning prisons over to it.[2] APAC is revolutionary in the arena of criminal justice and is a sign of the presence of God's kingdom in the world, not simply because people are visiting prisoners and caring for them, but because by their love and mercy for the marginalized, in their pursuit of justice, followers of Jesus are instruments in God's hands to make things right. Offenders are being restored, families reconciled, and the well-being of communities improved as the cycle of crime and violence is reduced.

Jesus portrays the kingdom of God by way of stories. In one story people are separated like goats from sheep. Jesus uses this story as a metaphor to depict righteous people being separated from the unrighteous. Those who are righteous are welcomed into God's kingdom, for they have responded to people like prisoners, the destitute, and the starving with mercy and compassion. Jesus provocatively tells his listeners that in caring for these people those who are righteous have been caring for him. Their righteousness is not one of moral purity, theological knowledge, prayers and devotion, or even good works alone, but of participation in God's ways of justice, mercy, and righting wrongs (peacemaking).

2. See chapter 8 for a story from one of the APAC-operated prisons.

MOVING IN THE SPIRIT

During the forty days after his death and resurrection, Jesus appears to the disciples and speaks to them about the kingdom of God.[3] On one occasion they ask Jesus a question about establishing a sociopolitical kingdom: "Lord, is this the time when you will restore the kingdom to Israel?"[4] Jesus responds, redirecting their question commissioning them to be his witnesses to the world. "But you will receive power when the Holy Spirit has come upon you; and you will be my witnesses in Jerusalem, in all Judea and Samaria, and to the ends of the earth."[5]

These are Jesus' final words to the disciples and echo the words he spoke in Nazareth at the beginning of his public ministry: "The Spirit of the Lord is on me, because he has anointed me to preach good news to the poor. He has sent me to proclaim freedom for the prisoners and recovery of sight for the blind, to release the oppressed, to proclaim the year of the Lord's favour."[6] The same Spirit who empowers Jesus to bring the good news of God's mercy and liberation to the poor and needy and captives is the Spirit who will empower his followers to bear that good news to the world.

The good news Jesus proclaims in word and deed represents total alignment with the will of the Father. Just as his words reflect total allegiance to the Father, so everything he has done is also in full accordance with the will and way of the Father. Jesus' parting commission is for his followers to continue that same witness, doing the Father's will as they move out into the world, in the power of the Holy Spirit.

It would be wrong to assume that Jesus commissions them only to preach and bear verbal witness in the world. Rather, he commissions them to be "all in." They are to proclaim the presence of God's kingdom by what they say and how they live. When the APAC groups go to prisons to care for inmates, their words and

3. Acts 1:3.
4. Acts 1:6.
5. Acts 1:7–8.
6. Luke 4:18–19.

presence and actions evidence the nearness of God's kingdom in the midst of human failure, inequity, injustice, and suffering.

WAY OF THE KINGDOM

Amid all the pressures and concerns of everyday life, Jesus challenges those who follow him to make the kingdom of God and his righteousness front and center in their lives.[7] Righteousness and kingdom are linked. The way of the kingdom is to seek and to submit to God's will and work of righteousness.[8] In love, when mercy and justice come together, there is peace and well-being, wrongs are righted, and relationships healed. In this the righteousness of God is made visible in our broken world.

God's love for humanity is expressed in compassion and mercy for needy, troubled people, and sinners like all of us. Jesus' proclamation of the good news of God's kingdom shows humankind the depths of the Father's love. Jesus calls his followers to do as he has been doing. Thus, when Jesus portrays the kingdom of God in the story of the sheep and the goats,[9] it is significant that those who feed the hungry, clothe the naked, and visit the prisoners are described as those who are righteous. They are considered righteous because amid all that has and is going wrong with humanity, they are instrumental in making things right. In the convergence of God's love and mercy and justice there is righteousness.

When the people of APAC reach out in compassion and friendship to prisoners, they are not reaching out to hapless offenders who deserve consideration, or who are asking for help, or even to those who are likely to respond positively. They are

7. Matthew 6:33.

8. See chapter 6 for a discussion on the righteousness of God in terms not only of perfection or holiness, but in terms of God's loving action to set right all that has gone so horribly wrong as consequence of human disobedience and rebellion—sin. God takes the initiative of rescuing humanity from the clutches of sin and restoring humankind to wholeness, a condition of flourishing and satisfaction.

9. Matthew 25:31–46.

JESUS: THE WAY OF GOD'S KINGDOM

reaching out to men and women who are made in the image of God yet are troubled and in trouble. They act to temper judgment with mercy so that justice will be done in righteousness.

Whenever we pray, "Our Father, who art in heaven, hallowed be thy name; thy kingdom come; thy will be done on earth as it is in heaven . . . ,"[10] there is a recognition that the coming of God's kingdom and doing God's will on earth are related. The kingdom of God is present and visible on earth in every witness to God's compassion and mercy for bruised and broken human beings. Whenever mercy and justice meet in love, the invisible kingdom of God is made visible. God's kingdom is not some otherworldly political geography, but is the domain of God's will and way for the salvation and restoration of humanity being enacted in the real world.

KINGDOM PEOPLE

New Testament writers use the image of citizenship in God's kingdom to encourage followers of Jesus in faithful and righteous living.[11] Citizens of God's kingdom are those who embrace God's rule in their lives. Paul tells the followers of Jesus in Corinth that they are ambassadors of Christ, ambassadors of God's redeeming and reconciling love in Jesus Christ:

> Christ's love compels us, because we are convinced that one died for all, and therefore all died. And he died for all, that those who live should no longer live for themselves but for him who died for them and was raised again. So, from now on we regard no one from a worldly point of view . . . Therefore, if anyone is in Christ, the new creation has come: The old has gone, the new is here! All this is from God, who reconciled us to himself through Christ and gave us the ministry of reconciliation: that God was reconciling the world to himself in Christ, not counting people's sins against them. And he has committed to us

10. Matthew 6:9–10.
11. Hebrews 11–12; Philippians 3; Ephesians 2.

the message of reconciliation. We are therefore Christ's ambassadors, as though God were making his appeal through us. We implore you on Christ's behalf: Be reconciled to God. God made him who had no sin to be sin for us, so that in him we might become the righteousness of God. As God's co-workers we urge you not to receive God's grace in vain.[12]

Everyone who embraces God's rule is a citizen of God's kingdom. Such citizenship implies more than a resident declaration of allegiance, it necessitates participation in God's loving "agenda" for the redemption and restoration of the world. Paul goes on to describe this participation as being co-workers with God as ambassadors of Christ, who are entrusted with both the message and the ministry of reconciliation.[13] Compelled by the love of Jesus Christ,[14] they embrace their God-given responsibility in both proclaiming the good news of reconciliation (the message) and being reconcilers (the ministry) in the world

Ambassadors reflect the heart of God's life-giving love for humanity. Having been reconciled to God (justified) by his unmerited love and grace and mercy, followers of Jesus (ambassadors) are so captivated by his love that they cannot look down on or exclude any other human being from God's mercy and justice. Contrary to what Paul describes as a "worldly point of view,"[15] that holds people's sins and faults against them, ambassadors of Christ regard and relate to all people in generous love as Jesus did. No one is beyond the margins or the reach of God's love and mercy and justice. God loves every human being without exception, and in the person of Jesus came not to judge the guilty but to reconcile all people to himself and to each other. This is the continuing work of God through citizens of God's kingdom, ambassadors of Christ.

Writing to followers of Jesus in Ephesus, Paul describes the change in their status as a complete change of allegiance from the

12. 2 Corinthians 5:14—6:1.

13. 2 Corinthians 5:18–19

14. 2 Corinthians 5:14.

15. 2 Corinthians 5:16.

kingdom of the world to God's kingdom of love and grace. This change of allegiance leads to a completely different way of living. Having been rescued from punishment and certain death, followers of Jesus understand the precious gift of grace and mercy, and God has given them a new way of living.

> As for you, you were dead in your transgressions and sins, in which you used to live when you followed the ways of this world and of the ruler of the kingdom of the air, the spirit who is now at work in those who are disobedient. All of us also lived among them at one time, gratifying the cravings of our flesh and following its desires and thoughts. Like the rest, we were by nature deserving of wrath. But because of his great love for us, God, who is rich in mercy, made us alive with Christ even when we were dead in transgressions—it is by grace you have been saved. And God raised us up with Christ and seated us with him in the heavenly realms in Christ Jesus, in order that in the coming ages he might show the incomparable riches of his grace, expressed in his kindness to us in Christ Jesus. For it is by grace you have been saved, through faith—and this is not from yourselves, it is the gift of God—not by works, so that no one can boast. For we are God's handiwork, created in Christ Jesus to do good works, which God prepared in advance for us to do.[16]

The NRSV translation sums it up this way: "For we are what he has made us, created in Christ Jesus for good works, which God prepared beforehand to be our way of life."[17] The good works of followers of Jesus do not earn them a place in God's kingdom, nor do good works of love, mercy, and justice make them righteous in the first place. All the good they do simply reflects God's grace, by which they have been justified and made righteous.

16. Ephesians 2:1–10.
17. Ephesians 2:10 (NRSV).

KINGDOM LIFESTYLE

Even during the worst of times of political turbulence, poverty, and illness, Gloria's ready smile and dark eyes sparkle with life. From the age of eighteen she knows that her vocation as a follower of Jesus is to love people in need or trouble. As a university student in Ecuador, she organizes a small group of like-minded students to offer legal, social, and spiritual support for men and women in prison. Reaching out to people in prison is both difficult and unpopular. Amid their own overwhelming social and economic need, prisoners are the least compelling, least deserving of all needy people. But Gloria persists, investing all her spare time and resources in doing what she can to care for and help them.

"God loves prisoners," says Gloria. "I am doing this with him."

In her mid-thirties Gloria is stricken with kidney disease. In spite of medical treatments, dialysis, and eventually a kidney transplant, her health does not improve. Eventually she is no longer able to keep her day job as a teacher, but she does not pull back from caring for prisoners.

"This is my real vocation," she says with a smile. "I must go to prison, Jesus is there."

During this time Gloria redoubles her efforts to advocate for the creation of a place in prison for inmates who wanted to change their lives and grow in faith. She is inspired by the story of APAC in Brazil. Though she is frequently rebuffed by prison officials and has little support from the community, Gloria remains undaunted and keeps pressing for change.

Her kidney transplant is failing and for three years Gloria's life alternates between her confinement in hospital and her visits to people in the confinement of prison. Her dream of creating a safe haven in prison for inmates who want to grow in faith and responsibility has been realized, but not without continuing obstacles. She spends every moment she can inside the small section of prison she calls APAC. But her strength is waning.

"Everyone wants to save my life," she says, "but the prisoners are my life."

Then, thirty-one years after her first visit to the prison, Gloria passes away. She was a most unusual woman whose life exuded her love for God and for people on the margins of her community.

Not every follower of Jesus is called to do what Gloria did, but every follower of Jesus is called to love beyond the limits of personal convenience and community approval. Loving like that is the lifestyle of God's kingdom. Just as singing the national anthem of a country does not make a person a citizen of that country, kingdom citizenship is not based on knowing theology, reciting the creeds, praying regularly, or attending church. Kingdom citizenship is about allegiance to Jesus Christ and walking in his way.

Jesus uses the image of a tree and its fruit to describe that allegiance to him is more than words of affiliation: "By their fruit you will recognize them. Not everyone who says to me Lord, Lord, will enter the kingdom of heaven, but only he who does the will of my Father in heaven.[18]"

Paul describes this fruit as the fruit of the Spirit, as opposed to the natural ways of self-interest, self-indulgence, and self-gratification: "The acts of the flesh are obvious: sexual immorality, impurity and debauchery; idolatry and witchcraft; hatred, discord, jealousy, fits of rage, selfish ambition, dissensions, factions and envy; drunkenness, orgies, and the like. I warn you, as I did before, that those who live like this will not inherit the kingdom of God. But the fruit of the Spirit is love, joy, peace, forbearance, kindness, goodness, faithfulness, gentleness and self-control. . . . Since we live by the Spirit, let us keep in step with the Spirit."[19]

LOVING GOD

In one of his last teachings Jesus sums it all up in "love." As God the Father loves him, so he loves his followers, and he enjoins them to love each other as he loves them. Loving others is the will of a loving God. Loving as God loves is not restricted to a circle of

18. Matthew 6:21.
19. Galatians 5:19–23, 26.

like-minded, friendly, "good" people. As evidenced in Jesus, God's love is expansive and inclusive. Loving as Jesus loves is to love those who are beyond the margins of social, political, and religious respectability. Jesus came to seek the last the least and the lost, those who need a "physician." Such love is not an armchair love of goodwill, it is to love like Gloria by putting one's self on the line, going the second mile, turning the other cheek, and going behind the bars of exclusion and rejection and judgment to embrace the troubled and the troubling. This is the fruit of a relationship with the loving God, encapsulated in Jesus' words to his followers.

> As the Father has loved me, so have I loved you. Now remain in my love. If you keep my commands, you will remain in my love, just as I have kept my Father's commands and remain in his love. I have told you this so that my joy may be in you and that your joy may be complete. My command is this: Love each other as I have loved you. Greater love has no one than this: to lay down one's life for one's friends. You are my friends if you do what I command . . . You did not choose me, but I chose you and appointed you so that you might go and bear fruit— fruit that will last . . . Love one another.[20]

Mercy and justice meet when those who follow Jesus put love into action by loving as Jesus loves. Love is the pivot. John's epistle eloquently emphasizes the centrality of love:

> Dear friends, let us love one another, for love comes from God. Everyone who loves has been born of God and knows God. Whoever does not love does not know God, because God is love . . . This is love: not that we loved God, but that he loved us and sent his Son as an atoning sacrifice for our sins. Dear friends, since God so loved us, we also ought to love one another.
> Dear friends, since God so loved us, we also ought to love one another . . . if we love one another, God lives in us and his love is made complete in us . . . And so we know and rely on the love God has for us. God is love. Whoever lives in love lives in God, and God in them . . .

20. John 15:9–14; 16–17.

We love because he first loved us. Whoever claims to love God yet hates a brother or sister is a liar. For whoever does not love their brother and sister, whom they have seen, cannot love God, whom they have not seen. And he has given us this command: Anyone who loves God must also love their brother and sister.[21]

The Letter to the Hebrews makes clear that "kingdom-love" extends beyond the comfortable borders of family and friends to include strangers and even prisoners: "Therefore, since we are receiving a kingdom that cannot be shaken, let us be thankful, and so worship God acceptably with reverence and awe . . . . Keep on loving one another as brothers and sisters. Do not forget to show hospitality to strangers, for by so doing some people have shown hospitality to angels without knowing it. Continue to remember those in prison as if you were together with them in prison, and those who are mistreated as if you yourselves were suffering."[22]

ADVANCING THE KINGDOM

The kingdom of God is not comprised of mere believers. It is comprised of believers who are "all in" with Jesus by embodying the good news of God's love for people, especially those on the margins. They are pilgrims by whose love, mercy, and justice are inextricably connected as much in their relationships with one another, as in welcoming strangers, caring for prisoners, protecting the vulnerable, caring for the sick, aiding the poor, upholding truth, and pursuing righteousness that brings peace, healing, and making things right. By this the kingdom of God is made visible and present in our broken world.

> Therefore, as God's chosen people, holy and dearly loved, clothe yourselves with compassion, kindness, humility, gentleness and patience. Bear with each other and forgive one another. If any of you has a grievance against someone. Forgive as the Lord forgave you. And over all these

21. 1 John 4:7, 8, 10–12, 16, 19, 20.
22. Hebrews 12:28; 13:1–3.

virtues put on love, which binds them all together in perfect unity. Let the peace of Christ rule in your hearts, since as members of one body you were called to peace. And be thankful. Let the message of Christ dwell among you richly as you teach and admonish one another with all wisdom through psalms, hymns, and songs from the Spirit, singing to God with gratitude in your hearts. And whatever you do, whether in word or deed, do it all in the name of the Lord Jesus, giving thanks to God the Father through him.[23]

The kingdom of God is being built, not by what we do for God, but by what God is doing in and through us. Nourished in God's love, in companionship with Jesus, in loving fellowship and worship with fellow believers, and empowered by the Holy Spirit, we reach out to embrace troubled, difficult, alienated, and needy people with the love of God. This is our God-given ministry and message as ambassadors of God's kingdom on earth.

PRISONS AND THE WORK OF THE KINGDOM: A SYNOPSIS

Why on earth should we care about criminals, convicts, and prisoners?

Simply put, we care because we believe in the God by whom every single human being is created in his image and is thereby endowed with dignity and worth. God loves the world of humanity, not just some of us. God is merciful to us and as recipients of his mercy we also are merciful. God is just, not merely judgmental: even when punishment is a consequence and punishment is necessary, God does not withdraw his love. God is righteous and calls us to righteous living; not as people who steer clear of "tax collectors and sinners" but as people who engage them as ministers of reconciliation, co-workers with God in setting things right.

The simple answer is that Jesus, who redeems and reconciles us to God, is our life. And when we go to prison to care for inmates,

23. Colossians 3:12–17.

and when we reach out in love to anyone who is reviled, or marginalized, or caught up in failure and disgrace—we will discover that Jesus is already there.

- Like Jesus of Nazareth, we are sent to the margins of our society to bring good news to outsiders and people in need.

- Like Jesus we are moved by God's grace to reach out in love to the most unlovable, unlikely, unbecoming of people, not because they are responsive, but simply because they are created by God in his image and God the Father sent him to love them, not to condemn them.

- We love because God loves us, because God is love, God is merciful, God is just, and God is righteous. It is the nature of God to rescue, redeem, reconcile, and restore bruised and broken people, victims and offenders, likeable and unlikeable people, and even enemies of the people.

- As Jesus came proclaiming and demonstrating the good news of the Father's unfailing love, we are compelled to express our love in action as well as in words.

- We are appointed by God as messengers and ministers of reconciliation. We are ambassadors of Christ and his kingdom.

- When we love as God loves us in Jesus, mercy and justice meet.

Without love there is no mercy.
Without mercy there is no justice.
Without justice there is no peace.

The symbol of the cross in the church points to the God who was crucified not between two candles on an altar, but between two thieves in the place of the skull, where the outcasts belong, outside the gates of the city. It does not invite thought, but a change of mind. It is a symbol which therefore leads out of the church and out of religious longing into the fellowship of the oppressed and abandoned.[24]

24. Moltmann, *Crucified God*, 40.

Bibliography

Arienda, Roger, and Marichelle Roque-Lutz. *Free Within Prison Walls.* Quezon City, Philippines: New Day, 1982.

Bunyan, John. *Pilgrim's Progress.* Brooklands Farm, UK: Ranso , 2020.

———. *The Unsearchable Riches of Christ.* John Bunyan Online Library. https://acacia.pairsite.com/Acacia.John.Bunyan/Sermons.Allegories/Sain.Know.Christ.Love/2.html.

Chesterton, G. K. "The Diabolist." https://www.gutenberg.org/files/8092/8092-h/8092-h.htm#link2H_4_0035.

Dostoevsky, Fyodor. *The Brothers Karamazov.* London: Heron, 1967.

Freedman, David Noel, Allen C. Beck, and Astrid B. Beck, eds. *Eerdmans Dictionary of the Bible.* Grand Rapids: Eerdmans, 2000.

Groarke, Louis. *Moral Reasoning.* London: Oxford University Press, 2011.

Koyama, Kosuke. *Three Mile an Hour God.* London: SCM, 2015.

Lamsa, George M., trans. *Holy Bible from the Ancient Eastern Text.* New York: Harper Collins, 1985.

Lewis, C. S. *The Weight of Glory.* New York: Harper Collins, 2001.

Moltman, Jürgen. *The Crucified God.* Minneapolis: Fortress, 1993.

Francis (Pope). *The Name of God is Mercy.* New York: Random House, 2016.

Rutledge, Fleming. *The Crucifixion: Understanding the Death of Jesus Christ.* Grand Rapids: Eerdmans, 2020.

Solzhenitsyn, Aleksandr I. *The Gulag Archipelago.* New York: Harper and Row, 1975.

Tse-Tung, Mao. *Quotations from Chairman Mao Tse-Tung.* Independently published, 2018.

Yancey, Philip, and Brenda Quinn. *Meet the Bible: A Panorama of God's Word.* Grand Rapids: Zondervan, 2000.

Yochelson, Samuel, and Stanton E. Samenow. *The Criminal Personality.* Lanham, MD: Rowman and Littlefield, 1985.

Subject Index

Scripture Index